※《탐라의 귀신》 책 이름의 '귀신'은 '천지귀신(天地鬼神)'의 의미다. 《삼국사기》,《삼국유사》,《고려사》,《조선왕조실록》 등에서 하늘과 땅 사이에 존재하는 모든 신령스런 존재들을 포괄할 때 쓰인다.

"신 등이 듣건대 '천지귀신(天地鬼神)의 이치는 가득 차 유동하는 것이라 사람과 간격이 없기 때문에 사람이 하는 일에 유통하지 않음이 없어, 선과 악을 지음에 따라 응하는 것이 마치 그림자나 울림과 같아 어기지 아니한다.' 하니 두렵지 아니하겠습니까? 임금이 된 이는 마땅히 천지귀신의 도리를 생각하고 자신이 지은 결과로 감응하는 이치를 살펴, 그 몸을 바르게 하고 덕을 닦아 정성을 다해 예로 섬기면, 천심을 받들고 신명을 협화(協和)시켜 어긋나거나 불순한 일이 없게 될 것입니다.—"

-《조선왕조실록》, 중종 13년(1518)

탐라의 귀신

톰 보렐리 지음

제주의 영원한 수호자들

In memory of my dear departed grandmother,
Rena Utterson (1925-2024)

들어가며

스무 살이 될 때까지만 해도 한국에 대해 생각해 본 적이 없었다. 한국에 살면서 한국 전통 신앙에 관련한 책에 관해서 쓰는 날이 올 줄은 상상도 못 했다. 어릴 때부터 여러 나라의 문화와 신화에 대한 관심이 많았지만, 한국 신화는 그 존재조차 몰랐었다. 대학에서 한국 근대사를 배우기 시작하면서부터 이 나라에 대해 조금 더 자세히 알 수 있었다.

한국에 와서 살게 된 2016년 여름까지도 근대 이전의 한국 역사나 전통 문화에 대한 지식은 전혀 없었다. 그러나 그해 말부터 삶에 큰 변화가 생겼다. 내가 머물렀던 익산의 어느 마을에는 운 좋게도 근처에 KTX역이 있었다. 한국의 철도는 매우 잘 되어 있어서 서쪽 전체를 쉽게 여행 다닐 수 있었다. 거의 주말마다 모험을 떠나 산골짜기에 자리 잡은 절과 소나무 숲 터에 숨어 있는 왕릉들을 둘러보았다. 익산에 머물며 삼국시대 때 익산을 지배했던 백제 역사에 푹 빠졌다. 이후 울산으로 이사한 후에는 삼국시대 신라의 유적지를 탐방하기 시작했다.

한국 역사와 전통을 공부하기 위해서 내가 넘어야 할 것은 지리적 경계가 아닌 언어적 경계였다. 이 주제를 다룬 영어로 된 책이 있었으나 대부분 수박 겉핥기식이었다. 책들은 한국 고유 전통 신앙보다는 외국에서 들여온 불교와 유교에 대해 중점적으로 설명하고 있었다. 하지만 나는 한국 고유 전통 신앙에 좀 더 관심이 갔다. 한국어로 된 책을 읽기 위해서는 한국어를 충분히 알아야 했다. 한국어를 익히는 것은 쉬운 일이 아니었다. 서울대학교 언어교육원에서 일 년 넘게 공부한 뒤 드디어 한국에 대한 책들을 읽을 수 있게 되었다. 그런데 아이러니하게도 처음 한국 전통 신앙에 관해 읽은 두 권의 책은 모두 번역본이었다. 일본의 민속학자 무라야마 지준이 쓴 《조선의 귀신》(1929)과 한국 민속학자 이능화가 한자로 쓴 《조선무속고》(1927)를 읽었다. 두 권 다 지금보다 한국 고유의 전통 신앙이 남아 있을 당시에 쓰인 책이었다. 나에게 이 두 권의 책은 그동안 접하지 못했던 활기차고 새로운 세상으로 가는 문을 여는 열쇠가 되어주었다. 책에서 묘사된 한국은 사람만큼이나 귀신과 신으로 가득 찬 곳이었다. 신들은 산과 바다, 마을과 주택의 각 방을 담당하고 있었고, 동물뿐 아니라 식물, 심지어 일상적인 물건에도 귀신이 깃들어 있었다. 책을 읽으면서 한국에도 고대 그리스 로마 신화만큼이나 무궁무진한 세계가 있고, 그들이 여전히 우리 곁에 있음을 깨닫게 되었다. 비록 오늘날 전통 가옥과 마을, 그리고 그곳에 깃들어 사는 신은 예전보다 줄었지만, 여전히 무속인을 통해 지금까지 전승되고 있다.

무속인들이 여전히 명맥을 이어가고 있지만, 옛날 사람들이 신들을 모셨던 유서 깊은 신당들은 빠르게 사라졌다. 특히 마을 신당들은 1970년대 새마을운동의 희생양이 되었다. 농촌 경제의 근대화를 위한 정책이었으나 한국 전통 종교들은 탄압과 파괴의 대상이 되었다. 지금은 한국 전통 무속신앙이 무형 문화유산으로 인정받고 있지만, 당시에는 근대화를 가로막는 해로운 미신으로 여겨졌다. 신령한 나무들이 베어졌고, 무속인들이 모시던 신들은 파괴되었다.[1] 오직 한국에서 가장 외진 지역이었던 제주만이 그 틈바구니에서 살아남았다.

제주에는 마을신을 모시는 신당이 영국 시골 마을의 교회만큼 흔하다. 그러나 내가 제주에서의 일자리를 제안받았을 때는 이러한 사실을 전혀 알지 못했다. 내가 제주에 대해 아는 것이라고는 다른 사람들이 알고 있는 정도로, 백사장과 귤 과수원으로 가득한 화산섬이라는 것뿐이었다. 이것으로도 제주에서 일을 할 이유는 충분했지만, 나를 제주에 머무르게 만든 것은 다른 데 있었다. 해변이나 과수원보다 매력적이었던 곳은 제주의 '신성한 숲'이었다. 요즘 내 낙은 섬 곳곳에 있는 사당(신당)에 가서 책으로만 읽었던 신의 얼굴을 직접 확인하는 일이다. 그러던 중, 제주의 신들이 위험에 처해 있다는 사실을 알게 되었다. 어떤 신당들은 방치된 채로 덤불에 잡아먹혔고, 또 어떤 곳은 건설 현장에 의해 사라졌다. 이 책이 미약하게나마 신당과 신당이 품고 있는 제주의 무형유산에 대한 인식을 확산하는 데 도움이 되기를 바란다.

한국에 처음 온 순간부터 지금까지 한국 사람들은 친절했고 나를 많이 도와주었다. 이 책과 카드 게임이 그 증거다. 동료 작가인 글지마와 연옥이 도와주었기에, 출판사

유물시선의 모든 분들이 내 작품이 빛을 볼 기회를 주었기에 이 모든 것이 가능했다.

지구 반대편에서 끊임 없이 격려해 주는 가족을 둔 것도 나의 큰 행운이다. 이 카드 게임을 처음 만들 때 도움을 준 형 제임스와 누나 에밀리, 어머니 헤더, 아버지 폴 등 가족에게도 감사를 전한다.

목 차

**1장.
무덤과 혼령 카드**
18

**2장.
무당 카드**
34

**3장.
유학자 목사 카드**
40

**4장.
뱀신 카드**
46

**5장.
가신 카드**
56

**6장.
죽음의 신 카드**
70

**7장.
마을신 카드**
80

8장.
제주 수호신과 공격신 카드
90

9장.
다산의 신 카드
102

10장.
농사의 신 카드
110

11장.
바다의 신 카드
118

12장.
도깨비 카드
130

제주, 공존의 섬
140

색인
154

誰從壁頂鑿灵沼
啣蛤幾廻貢貢鳥
拆峙山房果若然
奇觀問却知多少

蒼松绿竹紫檀香
赤栗乳柑橘柚黃
白雪丈餘紅綿樣
四時留得靑春光

누가 절벽 꼭대기에 신령스런 못을 파놓았는가
조개가 몇 번이나 입 벌리듯 새들만이 날아드네
우뚝한 봉우리 깎여 산방산 되었다는데 과연 그럴싸해
도리어 기이한 경관 물어 찾는 사람 많지 않네

짙푸른 솔과 푸른 대 그리고 자단향내
밤은 붉고, 유감, 귤, 유자는 노랗네
흰 눈이 한길 넘게 쌓여도 동백꽃 피어
사시사철 푸른 봄빛으로 머무르네

── 금남최부(錦南崔溥), '탐라시삼십오절' 중[2]

풍요의 섬, 제주

제주는 세계의 다른 어느 곳과 비교할 수 없는 독특한 매력을 지니고 있다. 그러나 '제주'라는 공식적인 명칭만으로는 이 섬의 진정한 정체성을 알기 어렵다. 제주(濟州)를 풀이하면 '물 건너에 있는 큰 고을'이다. 1294년 '제주'로 이름이 바뀌었고[3], 그 이전까지는 '섬나라'를 뜻하는 '탐라'로 불리었다. 섬의 특징을 잘 드러내는 표현들도 있다. 가장 유명한 표현으로 '삼다(三多)섬'이 있다. '삼다섬'은 바위, 바람, 여자가 풍요롭다는 뜻이다.

그러나 나를 매료시킨 제주도의 진정한 매력은 비물질적인 것에 있었다. 섬의 크기는 한국 전체 영토에 비해 작지만, 정신적 측면에서 이곳의 존재감은 크다. 제주는 보물

창고와 같다. 삼다섬에 하나의 풍요를 더한다면 무당들의 섬, '무당도'를 꼽고 싶다. 제주에는 250개의 신당, 400명의 무당, 500편의 무가[4], 1만 8천여 명의 신[5]이 있다. 그렇다고 섬 전체가 웅장한 사원과 신당으로만 뒤덮여 있는 것은 아니다. 제주 신들의 안식처는 일반적으로 작고 주변 환경과 어우러져 있다. 그 신성한 경계는 간소한 돌담일 뿐이며 신당을 드리운 튼튼한 폭낭(팽나무의 제주 방언)이 지붕을 대신한다. 이러한 간소함은 신성함을 부정하기는커녕 오히려 더 분명히 보여준다. 신당은 주변의 아름다운 풍경과 분리되어 있지 않고 어우러져 있다.

신당에 대해 알고 나면, 섬 전체가 신령스러운 기운으로 가득 찬 것처럼 느껴진다. 용왕이 해안을 보호하고, 바람의 신 '영등할망'의 숨결이 바다를 어루만진다. 울퉁불퉁한 화산 언덕 '오름'의 꼭대기에는 '산신'을 모시는 신당이 있고, 섬 중앙에 있는 화산에는 이 섬을 창조한 여신 '설문대할망'의 마지막 안식처가 있다. 원주민들은 단순히 자연에 감사하는 마음으로 신들을 믿은 것이 아니었다. 안타깝게도 이들의 믿음은 절망감에서 비롯되었다. 다른 어떤 것에도 의지할 수 없었던 상황에서 그들이 믿을 건 신 뿐이었다. 제주는 어떤 면에서는 풍요롭지만, 부족한 부분도 많았다. 특히 제주는 화산섬이어서 토양층이 매우 얇아 경작에 적합하지 않았다. 화산재 토양층으로 물이 빠르게 빠져나가 벼농사를 짓기 어려웠다. 이것이 바로 이 섬이 '삼재도'라고도 불리게 된 이유다. 제주의 삼재에는 '풍재(風災)', '수재(水災)', '한재(旱災)'가 있다.[6] 그러나 기후의 잔인성은 섬 바깥사람들이 행한 잔인함에 비하면 아무것도 아니었다. 역사 속에서 제주인들은 수많은 외세의 침략을 당했을 뿐만 아니라 한반도의 육지 사람들로부터 오랜 기간 경제적 수탈, 문화적 억압을 받았다.

  제주의 수많은 '신(神)'은 갑작스럽고 폭력적인 죽음으로 '귀(鬼)'가 된 이들이다. 귀신은 앞서 이야기한 네 개의 풍요에 더해, 제주의 다섯 번째 풍요를 담당한다. 앞으로 나올 이야기는 이 귀신과 신, 그리고 그들이 사는 공간에 대한 것이다. 책과 함께 52가지 제주 수호신 카드를 만들었는데, 이 책만 읽어도 괜찮다. 비록 짧은 글이지만 이 책을 덮을 때쯤 독자들이 나처럼 제주 고유의 신에 대한 감상을 얻기를, 그리하여 우리를 둘러싼 세계에 깃든 마법을 재발견하기를 바란다. 가장 평범한 장소와 물건에도 혼령이 깃들어 있다. 이를테면 집 안의 방, 커다란 나무가 드리우는 그늘 심지어 파도에 깎여나간 바위의 표면 하나하나에도.

1장.
무덤과 혼령 카드

산담
침입하는 뿌리
이장
뼈에 들끓는 벌레
벌초
조상원귀
한양일월
수명장자의 집

산담

조상 숭배 전통이 있는 한국에서 죽은 사람을 제대로 매장하는 일은 매우 중요했다. 시골길을 돌아다니기만 해도 어딜 가든 풀이 무성하게 자란 봉분이 있고, 반질반질 윤이 나는 검은색 묘비, 근엄한 표정의 무덤 지킴이 석상들을 볼 수 있다.

제주라고 예외는 아니다. 제주의 무덤은 일반적인 무덤과 달리 소위 무덤 벽이라고 할 수 있는 독특한 양식의 '산담'을 쌓았다. 산담을 통해 우리는 제주의 독특한 기후와 역사를 알 수 있다. 첫째, 산담은 동물들이 돌무더기를 짓밟거나 주위의 풀을 먹는 것을 막는 역할을 했다. 제주 땅은 수백 년간 소와 말을 기르는 목초지로 활용되었는데

소가 무덤을 망가뜨리면 무덤에 묻힌 조상들이 분노한다고 생각했다.[7] 둘째, 조선시대 제주에는 철이 귀해서 농기구를 만들 재료가 많지 않아 화전(火田)농업 방식이 발달하였는데, 그로 인해 불이 드는 것을 막기 위해서 산담을 쌓았다.[8] 셋째, 섬 곳곳에 널려 있는 수많은 화산암을 효율적으로 사용하기 위한 방법이었다.[9] 넷째, 섬 쪽으로 불어오는 매서운 바람으로부터 망자를 보호하기 위해서였다.[10] 산담은 바깥의 침입을 막기 위해 쌓은 벽이었으며, 그 안에 묻힌 영혼을 가두기 위해 쌓은 것이 아니었다.

영혼은 신문(神門)을 통해 자유롭게 드나든다. 신문은 산담 한쪽에 틈을 내어 귀신이 지나다닐 수 있도록 만든 문이다. 신문의 위치는 무덤 안에 있는 영혼의 성별에 따라 달라진다. 전통적으로 오른쪽은 음의 기운을, 위쪽은 양의 기운을 상징하여 여성의 무덤은 오른쪽에, 남성의 무덤은 왼쪽에 두었다.[11] 신문은 귀신이 사는 집의 정문이라고 할 수 있다. 신문에는 귀신들이 집으로 들어가기 전 신발을 벗어놓는 납작하고 평평한 돌을 놓았다.[12] '정돌'이라 불리며, 일종의 현관 역할을 한다. 무덤 봉분 앞에는 인석(人石)과 동자석 등의 동상을 세웠다. 인석은 조선왕릉에 모셔져 있는 문신상[13]과 유사하며, 사악한 기운을 막도록 했다.[14] 동자석은 제주 무덤에서 보이는 독특한 형태의 조각상이다. 동자석은 산담 안쪽에 세워둔 가장 작은 석상이며, 젊은 총각과 처녀의 모습을 하고 있어 '동녀'라고도 불린다. 이들은 무덤을 지키는 것이 아니라 망자의 심부름꾼 역할을 한다. 무덤 앞에 마주 보고 서 있다.[15]

한국에서는 전통적으로 죽은 자가 고통을 겪으면, 산 자도 고통스러워진다고 믿기 때문에 죽은 자를 보호하는 일이 중요했다. 조각상이나 담의 유무보다 더 중요한 것은 얼마나 좋은 위치에 무덤을 두느냐였다. 풍수지리에 따르면 땅 밑에는 생기가 흐르고 있는데, 기운이 충만한 곳에 묻히면 좋은 기운이 생긴다고 믿었다. 시신이 흡수한 기운이 후손에게 전해져 그들에게 복을 가져다 준다는 것이다.[16] 하지만 그러한 기운이 영원한 것은 아니며, 보통은 무덤에 묻혀있는 조상의 다음 4대~5대조까지 영향을 끼치고 이후에는 닿지 않는다고 생각했다. 일반적으로 뼈에 스며든 기운은 50~100년간 남아 있으며 뼈가 완전히 분해되면 기운도 사라진다.[17]

상서로운 곳에 매장을 하면 수십 년 동안 부와 건강을 얻을 수 있지만 불길한 곳에 잘못 묻히면 수십 년을 고통 속에 살 수도 있다. 조상을 기운이 부족한 지역에 모시거나 무덤을 방치하면 후손들은 무시무시한 대가를 치러야 한다. 불길한 징조는 병마로 나타났다. 무덤을 잘못 썼을 때, 혹은 무덤이 나무뿌리에 침범당했을 때, 조상이 '나병'을 저주로 내린다고 여겼다.[18] 해결책은 무덤을 옮기는 것이다. 육지에서는 이 과정을 '이장'이라고 하며, 제주에서는 '철리'라고 한다.[19] 땅을 파서 유해를 발굴했을 때, 뼈에 금이 갔거나 노랗게 변색되었다면 잘 씻어 맞추어 놓았다.

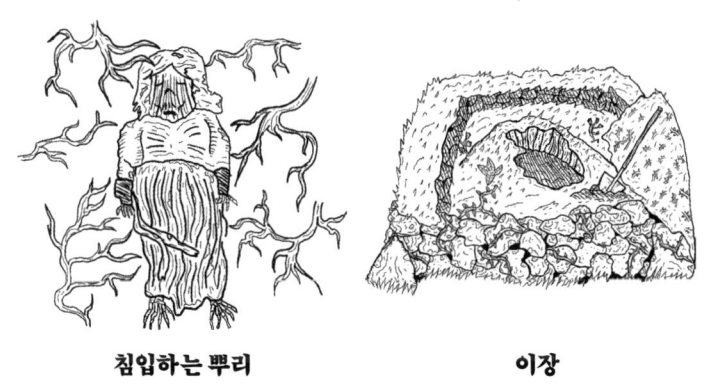

침입하는 뿌리　　　　　　**이장**

이장을 위해 특별히 고용된 뼈 맞추기 전문가도 있었다. 무덤을 파다가 뼈에 벌레가 우글거리는 것을 발견하면 더이상 이장 일을 하지 못하게 되었고, 빈곤과 질병으로 죽었다. 이는 가문의 종말을 알리는 징조였다.[20]

제주 사람들은 망자의 몸이 '땅귀'로부터 공격을 받는

다고 믿었다. 땅귀의 이름은 '삼두구미'로, 말 그대로 세 개의 머리와 아홉 개의 꼬리를 지녔다는 뜻이다. 다행히 삼두구미에게는 세 가지 약점이 있었으니 바로 달걀, 버드나무 가지, 그리고 쇠다. 철리 중에 이러한 물건들을 활용하여 시신을 보호했다.[21]

뼈에 들끓는 벌레   **벌초**

그러나 언제나 무덤을 옮기는 수고를 해야 하는 것은 아니었다. 위험으로부터 무덤을 보호하는 가장 간단한 방법으로 '벌초'가 있다. 벌초는 '풀을 베다'는 뜻으로 '벌(伐)'은 자르다, '초(草)'는 풀을 뜻한다. 벌초는 가족들이 조상의 묘를 정리하는 일이다. 낫으로 무덤의 풀을 다듬는 행위로, 전통적으로 남성 후손이 맡았다. 벌초는 한식날이나 추석 직전에 주로 했다. '한식(寒食)'은 동지로부터 105일째 되는 날이고[22], 추석은 음력 8월 15일로 한국의 추수감사절 같은 날이다. 제주에서는 음력 8월 1일에 벌초를 했는데, 2010년까지도 학교 공휴일로 지정될 정도로 중요한 날이었다.[23]

벌초는 중국에서 기원했다. 전설에 따르면, 진나라 진문공의 충직한 신하였던 개자추(介子推)의 비극적인 죽음을 기리고자 시작되었다고 한다. 진문공은 권력을 잡은 후 수년 동안 충신 개자추에게 감사하는 것을 잊었다. 이를 원망한 개자추는 조정에 나오길 거부하고 숲이 우거진 산 속에 들어가서 어머니와 살았다. 진문공은 개자추를 불러내기 위해 부하들에게 산불을 지르라고 명했다. 그러나 불길이 통제할 수 없을 정도로 커지는 바람에 개자추와 그의 어머니는 죽고 말았다. 자신의 부주의한 행동이 불러온 대가에 진문공은 크게 충격 받았다. 그는 개자추의 죽음을 기리기 위해 청명절을 만들었다. 영어로는 '무덤 청소의 날(Tomb Sweeping Day)'로 알려진 청명절은 조상의 묘를 다듬는 날이다. 청명절 축제는 단순히 원통한 개자추의 영혼을 달래는 것뿐만 아니라 비극적인 죽음을 맞이한 후 들판과 길가에 묻힌 영혼을 위로하는 의식이기도 했다.[24]

제주에는 '까마귀 모른 식게(제사)'가 있다. 이 의식은 음력 3월, 정월 삼짇날 조용히 소박하게 치러진다. 정식 제사처럼 대가족이 참여하지 않고, 오직 부모와 자녀들만 제사를 지낸다. '까마귀 모른 식게'는 후손이 없는 영혼을 위한 제사였다. 이승과 저승을 오가는 까마귀조차도 이 영혼들의 죽음에 대해 알지 못한다고 하여 '까마귀 모른 식게'라 이름 붙여졌다. 이 영혼들이 머물기 위해서는 낯선 이들에게 의지하는 방법밖에 없었다. 그렇다고 이들을 무시하면 큰일 난다. 불만을 품고 마을에 질병을 퍼뜨리기 때문이다. 집에서 멀리 떨어진 곳에서 비참하게 죽은 영혼을 '죽산이'라고 한다.[25] 그들은 원한을 품은 귀신인 '객귀' 또는 '원귀'가 된다. 갑작스럽게 죽음을 맞이했으니 저승으로 가는 길이 억울했을 것이 당연하다.[26] 제주에는 이런 영혼들이 아주 흔했다. 제주의 많은 남자들이 바다로 나갔다 죽었으며, 해적들에게 죽임을 당하거나 강제 노역에 시달리다가 죽었다. 제주에서의 삶이 얼마나 슬프고 가혹했는지 알 수 있는 지점이다.[27]

'손각시'[28]는 제주와 육지에 두루 많았던 미혼의 젊은 여성 귀신으로 조선시대에 특히 많았다. 조선시대에는 혼인한 여성의 혼령만 제사를 지내 주었다. 딸은 출가외인으로 여겨서 죽은 뒤에 남편 집안의 사당에 모셔졌다. 결혼 전에 죽으면 일종의 림보와 같은 곳에 갇혀 다음 생에 그들

조상원귀

의 조상과 함께 할 수 없으며, 이승의 자손들에게도 무시당했다.[29] 손각시는 어떤 '원귀'보다 두려운 존재였다. 이들이 위협적인 귀신이 된 것은 원한 때문만은 아니었다. 돌려받지 못한 사랑과 충족되지 않은 욕망이 산 자에 대한 증오심을 불러일으켰다. 혼인 전에 죽음을 맞이한 그들은 이성과 접촉할 수 있는 때가 없었다. 그들이 남성과의 접촉에 가장 많이 노출되는 때는 매장의 순간이었다. 젊은 여성들의 시신은 남성의 옷을 입힌 채 묻혀졌으며 번잡한 길목에서 남성의 발길에 짓밟히는 고통을 겪어야 했다.[30]

'고전적 조상 본풀이'에는 유독 끈질긴 손각시가 등장한다. 제주에서 온 문신 고전적이 한양에서 일할 적에 '한양일월'이라는 젊은 여인이 그에게 반했다. 그러나 고전적은 이미 결혼한 몸으로, 한양에서 벼슬 생활을 마치고 고향인 제주로 돌아갈 생각 뿐이었다. 한양일월은 고전적을 붙잡았지만 고전적은 냉정하게 뿌리치며 되려 여자의 뻔뻔함을 꾸짖었다. 한양일월은 고전적의 거절에 큰 충격을 받았다. 죽자마자 혼령이 되어 고전적의 집으로 쫓아갔다. 한양일월의 혼령은 여자들의 장신구를 보관하는 오색상자에 있는 옷가지에 달라붙어 제주의 해안까지 떠내려왔다. 그러던 중 고전적의 하인 '악생이'의 눈에 띄었다. 악생이는 그 안에 담긴 옷들을 보자마자 주인 아가씨가 이 옷을 입으면 얼마나 예쁠까 하는 생각이 들어 의심 없이 집으로 들고 갔다. 그런데 고전적의 딸이 그 옷을 입자 끔찍한 일이 벌어졌다. 거울에 비친 모습을 보며 감탄하던 중 갑자기 온몸이 떨리기 시작했고, 입에는 거품이 일었다. 한양일월의 혼령에 사로잡혀 정신을 잃고 만 것이다. 고전적은 소중한 딸이 그렇게 된 것을 보고, 무당에게 조언을 구했다. 무당은 광증의 이유와 치료 방법을 알려주었다. 혼령을 내쫓는 굿판을 벌여 한양일월의 혼령이 그토록 갈망했던 애정을 주어야 했다. 양반인 고전적은 그 방법이 내키지 않았지만 어쩔

한양일월

수 없었다. 그러나 이것으로도 충분하지 않았는지 7일 후 고전적의 딸은 죽음을 맞이했다. 상심에 빠진 고전적과 그의 하인도 얼마 지나지 않아 숨을 거두었다. 그 소식을 들은 무당마저 몸을 떨기 시작하더니 결국 쓰러져 다시는 일어나지 못했다.[31]

'천지왕 본풀이'에는 하늘과 땅의 왕 '천지왕'이 등장한다. 그는 세상의 첫 번째 통치자였다. 사람들이 평화롭고 조화롭게 살아갈 수 있도록 도왔다. 하늘과 땅이 화합하는 평화로운 세상을 위해 하늘의 남자 천지왕은 아내를 찾으러 땅으로 내려왔다. 그가 가장 중요하게 생각했던 아내의 자질은 미모나 재력이 아니라 지혜였다. 온 땅을 샅샅이 뒤지던 중 어떤 한적한 마을에서 '총명'이라는 이름의 어인을 발견했다. 천지왕은 총명의 부모에게 혼인 허락을 구했으나, 부모는 딸의 결혼에 지참금을 많이 줄 수 없다며 자신들의 처지를 부끄러워했다. 총명의 집에는 소박한 혼인 잔치에 쓸 쌀조차 없었다.

총명의 부모는 '수명장자'의 집을 찾아갔다. 수명장자는 마을에서, 어쩌면 이 세상에서 가장 부자인 사람이었다. 그는 힘이 장사여서 상대가 사람이든, 짐승이든, 혹은 신이든 그 어떤 것과도 맞설 자신이 있었다. 수명장자에게 두려움이란 없었다. 원하는 것은 무엇이든 할 수 있었으며, 지배욕과 권력욕을 남용했다. 사람들은 수명장자에게 공물을 바치느라 먹고살기에도 빠듯할 지경이 되었다.

수명장자는 문간에서 쌀을 구걸하는 총명의 부모를 발견했다. 수명장자는 다른 마을 사람들 대하듯 그들에게도 똑같이 했다. 수명장자로부터 비싼 흰 쌀을 받아온 총명의 부모는 집에 돌아와 쌀의 상태를 확인해 보았다. 쌀에는 모래가 뒤섞여 있었다. 그러나 가진 음식이라고는 이 쌀밖에 없었던 부부는 쌀에서 모래알을 골라내는 수밖에 없었다. 아홉 번이나 헹궈내도 깨끗이 걸러지지 않았다. 천지왕이 첫술을 떴는데 거친 모래가 씹혔다. 화가 난 천지왕은 총명의 부모를 불러들였다. 부부는 이 모든 일이 수명장자 때문이라며, 수명장자가 너무 많은 문제를 일으키고 있다고 고했다. 부부의 이야기를 듣고 흥미가 생긴 천지왕은 수명장자에 대해 조금 더 자세히 말해 보라고 했다. 이야기를 들을수록 천지왕은 화가 치밀어 올랐다. 수명장자는 사람들을 협박하였고, 온갖 속임수로 막대한 부를 축적하는 수전노였다. 가난한 사람들이 쌀을 달라고 하면 하얀 모래를 섞어 주고, 수수밥을 달라고 하면 검은 모래를 섞어 주었다. 줄 때는 적게 주고, 받을 때는 많은 것을 요구했다. 그의 자식들도 똑같았다. 수명장자의 딸들은 밭에서 잡초를 뽑는 일꾼에게 썩은 간장만 주고, 신선한 간장은 자기들끼리만 먹었다. 아들들은 소와 말에게 주는 물도 아까워 말 발굽에 오줌을 누어 마치 말들이 이미 물을 마신 것처럼 보이게 하는 괘씸한 행동을 저질렀다. 천지왕은 사람과 짐승에 대한 동정심이 없는 그런 자들은 살아있을 자격이 없다고 생각했다. 천지왕은 수명장자 집안에 세 명의 장군 '벼락장군', '우뢰장군', '화덕장군'을 보냈다.

이후 벌어지는 이야기는 여러 버전이 있다. 수명장자와 그의 가족이 벼락에 맞아 집은 불타고 즉사했다는 설, 수명장자가 끝까지 싸워 많은 천지왕의 병사들을 죽이긴 했으나 그전에 제압당하였다는 설도 있다. 어쨌든 수명장자와 그의 가족이 전부 처참한 최후를 맞이했다는 결말은 똑같았다. 하지만 그들은 원귀가 되어서도 문제를 일으켰다. 그들을 원한을 품은 최초의 '원귀'로 보며, 무당들이 이때부터 굿을 하기 시작했다고 한다. 죽은 사람들의 원혼을 달래기 위해 신당 뒤편에 제물을 바치는 풍습이 생겼으며, 불이 날 때마다 '화덕장군'에게 '불찍굿'을 올리는 풍습이 생겼다. 일부 기록에서는 수명장자 일가가 다양한 동물로 환생했다고 언급되어 있다. 천지왕은 인간이라면 저지를 수 없는 그들의 잔인한 행위에 형벌을 내렸다. 하인들에게 제대로 된 음식을 주지 않았던 수명장자의 딸들은 곡물을 파먹는 '팥벌레'가 되었다. 가축에게 물을 주지 않았던 수명장자의 아들들은 솔개로 변했다. 솔개들은 깃털에 고인 빗물만을 먹으며 영원히 갈증에 시달렸다.[32]

수명장자의 집

2장.
무당 카드

심방
영집
삼멩두

심방

한국의 무당들은 원한을 품은 영혼을 쫓아내는 데 가장 뛰어난 전문가다. 그들은 수천 년 동안 원혼들이 다음 생으로 나아갈 수 있도록 돕는다. 하지만 퇴마는 그들이 수행하는 많은 역할 중 하나에 불과하다. 그들은 치료사이자 점쟁이였으며 길한 것을 불러들이고 제물을 바치는 제사장이기도 했다.[33]

제주에서는 무당을 '심방'이라고 부른다. 무아지경에 오른 자, 신과 가까운 자[34], 신의 심부름꾼, 신의 자식 등 다양한 의미가 담겨 있다.[35] 또는 '신의성방'으로 불리는데 신과 대화를 나누는 최초의 사람이라는 뜻이다.[36] 육지의 무당들처럼 도구를 활용하여 '굿'을 한다. 굿이란 다양한 요소들로 구성된 복합적인 무속 의식으로, 신에게 축복을 빌고 해로운 귀신을 쫓아내는 노래, 춤, 극적인 낭송 등의 퍼포먼스로 구성된다.[37] 죽은 사람을 다음 생으로 안전하게 인도하여 유족들이 마지막 작별인사를 할 수 있도록 해준다. 굿의 핵심 요소는 '본풀이'다. '본'은 기원(本)을, '풀이'는 해결 또는 풀이를 뜻한다. 본풀이는 신의 기원에 관한 이야기다.[38] 본풀이는 제주굿에서 가장 중요하다. 신이 어떻게 지금의 지위를 얻게 되었고, 어떤 이유로 숭배받게 되었는지 알려준다. 심방은 본풀이를 읊으며 신을 즐겁게하고, 때로는 아첨하여 원하는 소원을 들어주도록 유도한다.[39]

심방의 도구는 의식의 시작부터 끝까지 중요한 역할을 한다. 이 도구를 '기메'라고 부른다. 기메의 한 가지 흥미로운 예로 '영집'이 있다. 영집은 '영혼이 와서 머무는 집'으로 길 잃은 혼령을 위한 휴식 공간이자 위로의 장소다. 흔히 '무혼굿'에서 많이 쓰인다. 무혼굿이란 바다에서 익사한 사람들이 저승에 안전히 갈 수 있도록 보내주는 의식을 말한다. 장례를 치러줄 사람이 없는 이들은 한이 많다. 무혼굿을 할 때, 망자를 상징하는 인형에 망자의 옷을 입히고 이불을 덮어주며 병풍을 쳐서 모신다. 그 위로 메밀이나 쌀

영집

가루를 뿌리고 영집을 덮어 놓는다. 필요한 기물과 제물이 준비되면 심방은 고인이 전생에서 벗어나 환생할 수 있도록 기원한다. 심방은 굿이 끝나면 영집을 걷어내고 그 안의 가루를 살핀다. 영혼이 새로 환생했다면 가루 안에서 새 발자국 같은 상징이 나타나고, 나비로 변했다면 나비 날개와 같은 상징이 나타난다.[40]

    제주의 심방들은 '삼멩두'라 부르는 신물을 갖고 있다. 삼멩두는 다음의 세 가지 도구를 지칭한다.

❶ 신칼: '시왕대번지'라고 불리는 일종의 신성한 칼.
❷ 산판: '天(천)', '地(지)' '門(문)' 세 개의 한자가 새겨진 엽전 모양의 천문 한 쌍과 술잔 모양의 작은 놋그릇 상잔 한 쌍, 천문과 상잔을 담는 접시 모양 놋그릇 산대가 하나의 조합을 이룬다.
❸ 요량[요령]: 오색천으로 꾸민 작은 놋쇠 방울.[41]

신칼, 산판, 요량의 삼멩두는 각각 제주 무속 조상신 삼형제 본맹두, 신맹두, 삼맹두를 형상화한 것이다.[42] 이 기메들을 통칭하여 '조상'이라고 부르기도 한다. 기물은 무당에서 무당으로 전승되는데, 기물에는 이전에 사용했던 무당들의 영혼이 깃든다고 믿었다.

3장.
유학자 목사 카드

이형상 목사
양씨 목사
천구아구대멩이

이형상 목사

무당들이 한국 사회에서 늘 환영받는 것은 아니었다. 조선시대 무당은 사회에서 가장 낮은 천민 계층으로 강등됐다. 조선에서는 성리학을 엄격히 고수하였고, 무당을 평민들 사이에 천박한 미신을 퍼뜨리는 사기꾼으로 깎아내렸다. 고려시대 때도 무당이 국가 제사에서 배제되긴 하였지만[43], 조선시대에는 백성들이 사는 마을에서까지 배제되었다. 무당들은 푸줏간이나 대장장이로 일하던 사람들과 함께 천민으로 여겨져 마을에서 동떨어진 곳에서 살아야 했다.[44] 유교 사상에 따르면, 하늘의 명을 받을 수 있는 사람은 오직 왕뿐이었다. 그들은 왕인 동시에 제사장으로, 나라의 번영을 위해 공식 제단에 혼령(신)들을 위한 제물을 바쳤다. 왕 외에 여러 관료들도 의식을 수행하는 임무를 맡았다. 이들에게 무당은 위계질서를 무너뜨리는 존재였다. 그러나 조선에서 지리적으로 멀리 떨어져 있던 제주의 무당들은 상대적으로 국가의 규제에서 자유로웠다.[45]

1702년 이형상이 제주의 새로운 목사로 임명되면서 상황이 달라졌다. 그는 유교를 전파하여 섬의 종교적 질서를 바로잡고자 했다. 이형상 목사가 보기에 제주의 제례는 '비도덕적인 의식[46]'이었고, 부정한 귀신에게 지내는 '음사(淫祀)[47]'였다. 조선의 국가 의례 매뉴얼이 담긴 '사전(祀典)'에 실리지 않은 비공식적인 제사였다.[48] 그는 섬의 '음사'를 없애기 위해 몇몇 사찰과 최소 129곳 이상의 신당을 훼손하였다.[49] 그러나 승리를 자축할 시간은 길지 않았다. 그가 속한 당파 세력이 약해지자 이형상 목사는 1703년 파직당했다.[50] 후임으로 온 이희태 목사는 이형상이 이룬 업적들을 되돌리기 시작했다. 이희태는 제주에 도착하자마자 성대하게 신을 기리는 제사를 지냈으며, 심방에게 파괴된 신당을 재건하라고 명했다.[51]

비록 목사로 지낸 기간은 짧았지만, 이형상 목사가 제

주에 남긴 흔적은 상당하다. 다양한 전설에서 이형상은 여러 신들과 대결을 벌인 인물로 묘사된다. 그중 하나로 '광정당신'이 있다. 구전되는 이야기에 따르면, 이 신은 커다란 뱀의 형상을 하고 있다. 안덕면에 있는 신당에서 광정당신이 나오는 것을 본 이형상은 병사를 시켜 그 자리에서 죽였다.[52]

뱀신과 유교 남성의 대립이 제주에서만 있던 것은 아니었다. '토산 본풀이'는 전남 나주에서 시작된다. 옛날 나주에 새로운 목사들이 부임한 날에 바로 죽는 일이 연달아 일어났다. 당연히 아무도 그 자리를 맡고 싶지 않았다. 그러던 중 용감한 한 사람이 나섰다. '양씨'라 불리는 남자였다. 그는 곧바로 나주로 향했다. 나주에 들어와 금성산을 지날

양씨 목사

무렵이었다. 수행원들은 이 산에서 신기가 느껴진다며 양씨에게 말에서 내리라고 했다. 이대로 말을 타고 있다가는 산신을 노하게 할 것이라며 두려워했다. 하지만 양씨는 그런 미신에 굴복하지 않았다. 겁에 질린 부하들을 달래며 꿋꿋이 말을 타고 산을 올랐다. 일행은 산을 오르던 중 청기와집 하나를 우연히 발견했다. 양씨가 말에서 내려 안마당으로 들어갔더니 아름다운 여인이 그를 맞이하고 있었다.

"당신은 사람입니까? 아니면 귀신입니까? 당신의 진짜 정체는 무엇입니까?"

양씨는 그녀의 매력에 빠져들지 않은 채 단호히 물었다. 그러자 여인이 무언가로 변하기 시작했다. 어느새 그 자리엔 여인이 아닌 뱀 한 마리가 자리하고 있었다. 윗아가리는 하늘에 닿고 아래 아가리는 땅에 닿을 정도로 거대한 뱀의 모습을 하고 있었다. 여인의 정체는 '천구아구대멩이' 귀신이었다. 양씨의 부하들은 비명을 지르며 흩어졌다. 하지만 양씨는 침착하게 장검을 꺼내 겁 없이 뱀의 목을 베었다. 그러고는 부하들을 시켜 불을 지르게 했다. 집은 순식간에 불에 타 재로 변했다.[53]

천구아구대멩이

4장.
뱀신 카드

~~~~~~~~~~~~~

칠성신상과 허멩이 인형

방울품

안칠성

고팡

칠성신상과 허멩이 인형

제주에서는 뱀을 수백 년 동안 숭배해왔다. 1520년 제주에 유배되었던 학자 김정이 펴낸 《제주풍토록》에는 '높은 기온과 습도로 인해 섬에 뱀이 득실거렸다'고 나와 있다. 그러나 주민들은 뱀을 저주가 아닌 숭배의 대상으로 여겼다. 뱀을 마주쳐도 쫓아내지 않고, 기도를 외우고 술을 바쳤다.[54] 뱀은 다른 사납고 위험한 동물들과 달리 울타리 안이나 벽, 심지어 초가집 지붕 등 인간 가까이에서 함께 사는 것을 선택했다. 섬사람들은 뱀을 두려워하기보다 함께 살아가는 친근한 생명체로 여겼다.[55] 그렇기에 당연히 뱀을 죽여야 하는 대상으로 상상할 수 없었다. '죽은 뱀을 보면 눈이 먼다', '죽은 뱀을 만지면 손이 썩는다'는 등의 속설도 있다. 뱀 영혼은 자기를 죽인 사람에게 분노하여 저주를 내리는 방식으로 복수한다. 그러나 뱀은 자신을 죽인 사람을 다른 사람으로 착각하여 잘못 저주를 내리기도 했다. 뱀의 저주를 받은 사람들은 뱀처럼 혀를 날름거렸고 피부는 뱀의 비늘처럼 변했으며 뱀이 닿은 부위에 통증이 나타났다.

저주를 치료할 유일한 방법은 '칠성새남굿'을 치르는 것이었다. 칠성새남굿은 '허멩이 놀림'으로 구성된다. 허멩이 놀림은 누군가가 뱀을 죽이는 모습을 보고 그 죄를 뒤집어 써서 억울하게 저주를 받게 된 환자가 뱀을 죽인 자를 찾아가 죄를 물으며, 환자가 죄인이 아니었음을 밝혀내는 과정이다. 죽은 뱀을 다시 살리는 과정을 연출하는데, 이때 뱀을 진짜로 죽인 자를 상징하는 '허멩이 인형'을 만들어 사용한다. 이들은 겉으로는 양반 행세를 하지만, 불을 지르며 온갖 재앙을 일으키는 악신들이다. 허멩이 놀림에서 심방은 재판관 역할을 한다. 허멩이 인형을 엎드리게 하고 곤장을 쳐서 자백을 받는다. 그러면 인형 안에 있는 영혼은 각다귀섬으로 추방된다. 각다귀란 모기처럼 남의 피를 흡혈하는 곤충류들을 말한다. 남의 것을 뜯어먹고 사는 사람을 이르는 말로도 쓰인다. 뱀이 이 모든 과정을 볼 수 있도록, 뱀을 상징하는 '칠성신상(七星神像)' 종이 인형도 만든다. 허멩이가 자백하여 벌을 받는 것을 보고 분노에서 벗어난 뱀의 영혼은, 환생할 준비를 하며 뱀의 죽음을 본 사람은 저주에서 풀려난다.[56] 제주에서 뱀과 칠성신은 밀접한 관련이 있다. 칠성신은 수천 년 동안 한국에서 숭배되었고, 인간의 운명을 결정짓는 존재로 여겨졌다.[57] 7명의 칠성신은 우리 삶에 제각기 다른 방식으로 영향을 미친다. 어떤 신은 재난을 관장하고, 어떤 신은 우리의 수명을 결정한다.[58] 앞으로 만나게 될 뱀신 중에는 아예 '칠성신'이라는 이름으로 불리는 신도 있다.

죽은 뱀의 저주를 푸는 또 다른 방법으로 '방울품'이 있다. 이 의식은 두 번이나 연달아 폭력적인 죽음을 맞이했던 뱀의 영혼을 달래고자 시작되었다. 첫 번째 죽음은 앞서 보았듯 양씨의 손에서 비롯되었다. 양씨는 몰랐겠지만 사실 그때 뱀은 죽은 게 아니었다. 그것은 다른 형태로 살아남았다. 나주로 향하던 양씨가 죽인 뱀은 금바둑돌과 옥바둑돌로 변해 서울 종로 네거리로 떨어졌다. 바

방울품

둑돌은 서울에 진상품을 바치러 가던 제주의 강씨 형방, 오씨 형방, 한씨 형방의 눈에 띄었다. 세 형방은 바둑돌을 주운 뒤 가던 길을 갔다.

일을 마치고 돌아오는 길, 세 형방은 신기해 보였던 바둑돌이 영 대단하지 않은 듯하여 길바닥에 다시 던져버렸다. 이것은 실수였다. 그들은 그때까지만 해도 바둑돌이 그들의 순조로운 여정을 도왔다는 사실을 알지 못했다. 세 형방이 항구에 도착하자, 강한 바람이 불어와 그들을 밀어냈다. 어떻게 해야 할지 몰라 당황한 세 형방은 유명한 무당을 찾아갔다. 무당은 그들이 아직 돌 하나를 가지고 있으며, 집으로 돌아가기 위해서는 돌을 위한 굿을 먼저 해야 한다고 말했다. 그렇게 해야만 바람이 바뀔 것이라고 했다.

세 형방은 그 말을 듣고 바둑돌을 모시고 굿을 했다. 제주에 배가 도착하자 바둑돌은 아기씨로 변해있었다. 아기씨는 사람들이 알아차리지 못하는 사이에 스르르 먼저 배에서 내렸다. 그러나 뭍에 내린 아기씨에게 토지관이 나타나 말했다. 한 마을에 토지관이 둘일 수 없으니 '토산리'로 가라는 것이다. 토산리에 도착한 아기씨는 이곳에 좌정하기로 마음먹었다.

그러나 이곳도 위험하긴 마찬가지였다. 아기씨와 그의

하녀가 바닷가에 있는 용천수에서 빨래하던 중이었다. 왜놈들이 탄 배가 나타나 그들을 습격했다. 아기씨와 하녀들은 왜놈에게 몸을 더럽혔다고 생각해 그대로 세상을 등졌다. 마을 사람들이 두 여자의 시신을 발견하였고 원한이 깃든 영혼을 달래기 위해 쌍둥이 무덤을 만들어주었다. 그러나 토산리 자손들 아무도 그들을 신으로 대접해 주지 않았다. 아기씨는 화가 나 마을의 어린 여성들에게 화를 입히기 시작했다. 소녀들의 몸에 빙의하여 몸을 통제하지 못하게 만들기도 했다. 결국 사람들은 마을의 심방을 찾았다. 심방은 귀신 들린 소녀들이 불행해진 원인을 찾고자 '방울풂'을 하기 시작했다.[59] 심방은 아기씨의 원한을 풀기 위해 종이에 뱀 형상을 그리고, 방울 모양의 명주 매듭을 묶었다. 심방은 이것을 소녀들의 몸에 붙였다. 그리고 매듭을 풀어 '방울아기씨'의 원한을 풀어주자, 소녀들은 빙의에서 풀려났다. 이 의식은 섬 전역으로 퍼졌다.[60]

원한을 푼 아기씨는 친절한 신이 되었다. 한때 해를 입었던 젊은 여자들은 이제 어디에 있든 아기씨로부터 보호받는 존재가 되었다. 심지어 마을의 여자들은 혼인할 때, 아기씨에게 제례를 올렸다. 마당에 작은 동굴 '칠성눌'을 지어 모셨다.[61] 섬 주민들은 뱀신인 방울아기씨에게 깊은 존경심을 표했으며, '안칠성'과 함께 모셨다. 안칠성 역시 방울아기씨와 유사하고도 충격적인 기원 이야기를 품고 있다.

안칠성은 원래 중국의 어느 귀족 집안의 딸이었다. 어린 나이에 한 승려에게 납치되었다가 겨우 집에 돌아왔는데, 부모는 돌아온 딸이 임신한 것을 보고 경악했다. 명망 있는 양반 집안으로서 견딜 수 없는 수치라며 딸을 무쇠 상자에 가둬 동쪽 바다에 띄워 버렸다. 바다를 떠돌던 무쇠 상자는 어찌어찌해서 제주 해안까지 떠밀려 왔다. 그녀는 기적적으로 살아남았을 뿐만 아니라 일곱의 건강한 딸들도 낳았다. 그러나 안타깝게도 그녀와 아이들 전부 뱀으로 변해 버렸다. 어미뱀은 토산본풀이의 아기씨처럼 자신을 숭배해 줄 사람을 찾아다녔다. 그들을 뱀 이상의 존재로 대우해 준 첫 번째 사람은 송대정부인이었다. 송대정부인은 뱀

안칠성

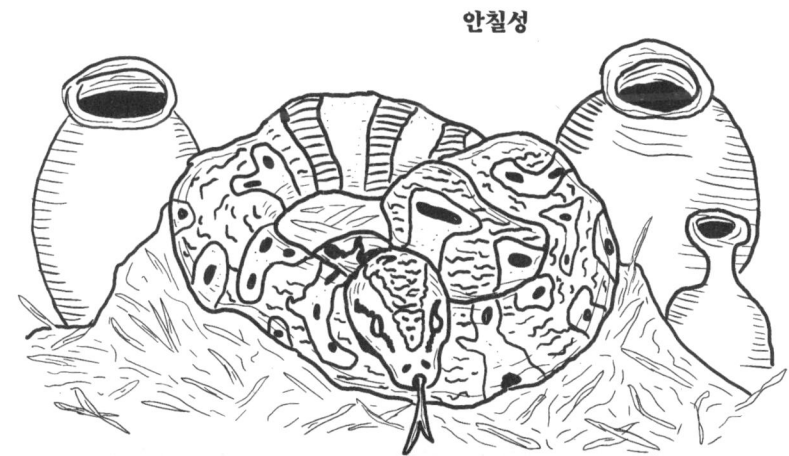

을 보고 조상신일 수도 있다고 생각하여 조심스럽게 집으로 데려와 고팡에 모셨다.

얼마 후 어미 뱀은 딸들을 불러 모았다. 그녀는 이 집안의 제물은 언젠가 동이 날 것이기 때문에, 더 이상 한집에 살 수 없다고 말했다. 딸들에게 어느 곳에 좌정할 것인지 물었다. 딸들은 각자 한 군데씩 선택해 그곳을 맡아 신이 되었다.

❶ 큰딸은 추수못(제주시 삼도동에 있었던 못)을 차지하여
추수칠성신이 되었다.
❷ 둘째딸은 이방(吏房)·형방(刑房)을 차지하여
이방형방칠성신이 되었다.
❸ 셋째딸은 옥(獄)을 차지하여
옥지기칠성신이 되었다.
❹ 넷째딸은 동과수원과 서과수원을 차지하여
과원칠성신이 되었다.
❺ 다섯째 딸은 동쪽과 서쪽의 창고를 차지하여
창고지기칠성신이 되었다.
❻ 여섯째는 광청못(제주시 삼도동에 있던 못)을 차지하여
광청칠성신이 되었다.
❼ 가장 효녀였던 일곱째는 집 후원 귤나무 밑을 차지하여

귤을 진상 받아 어머니께 올렸고, 밧칠성신이 되었다.

어미 뱀은 고팡을 맡아 곡식을 지키겠다고 말했다. 이후 어미 뱀은 안칠성으로 불리게 되었다.[62] 칠성신은 신격화된 일곱 별, 한국말로 '북두칠성'을 뜻한다. 한국에서 북두칠성은 수천 년 동안 모든 인류의 운명을 관장하는 것으로 믿어져 왔다. 제주의 안칠성은 칠성신의 축소판이다. 칠성신이 인류 전체의 운명을 관장한다면, 안칠성은 한 집안의 운명을 관장한다.

고팡

5장.
가신 카드

주목지신
정주목과 정낭
노일제대귀일의 딸
정지(부엌)
조왕할망
문전신
상방

주목지신

제주 전통 가옥에는 뱀뿐만 아니라 여러 신이 깃들어 있다. 구석구석에 수많은 신이 있다. 우리에게 흔히 알려진 가정신들 대부분은 '문전 본풀이'에 등장한다.

남선비와 그의 아내 여산부인에게는 일곱 아들이 있었다. 남선비 가족은 가난했지만 행복했다. 그러나 '노일제대귀일의 딸'이 새식구로 들어오면서 문제가 생기기 시작했다. 노일제대귀일의 딸은 탐욕스럽고 교활한 인물로, 남선비가 쌀을 팔러 오동나라에 갔다가 만난 여인이다. 남선비는 노일제대귀일의 딸에게 속아 돈을 몽땅 탕진했다. 집으로 돌아갈 수 없을 정도로 가난해진 그는 어쩔 수 없이 그녀와 두 번째 혼인을 하게 된다. 그녀는 남선비에게 더 이상 가져갈 돈이 없자, 그의 기운을 빼앗기 시작했다. 남선비에게 죽지 않을 만큼의 쌀겨죽만 먹였다. 급기야 남선비는 눈이 멀었다.

 3년이 지난 후 여산부인은 소식 없는 남편이 걱정되어 찾아 나섰다. 겨우 남선비를 찾았지만 노일제대귀일의 딸이 가만히 있을 리 없었다. 노일제대귀일의 딸은 여산부인을 속여 주천강으로 유인한 후, 가장 깊은 곳으로 밀어 넣어 익사시켰다. 돌아와서는 자기가 여산부인인 척하였다. 여산부인의 목소리를 흉내 내며 노일제대귀일의 딸이 어떻게 죽었는지 설명했다. 남선비는 이 소식을 듣고 기뻐하며 아들들이 있는 원래 살던 집으로 함께 돌아가자고 했다.

 남선비의 아들들은 아버지처럼 쉽게 속지 않았다. 아들들은 어머니의 외모가 너무 달라져 있어 낭황해했다. 어떻게 된 일이냐고 묻자, 노일제대귀일의 딸은 그동안 너희의 아버지를 찾느라 고생해서 이렇게 변했다고 얼버무렸다. 그러나 금방 자신의 정체가 들통날 것을 예감한 노일제대귀일의 딸은 여산부인의 아들들을 없앨 계획을 세웠다. 그녀는 병에 걸린 척하며, 남선비에게 일곱 아들의 간을 먹는 것이 유일한 치료법이라고 말했다. 다행히 아들들이 그 말을 엿듣고 있었다. 똑똑한 막내 '녹디성인'이 나름대로 계책을 생각해 냈다. 돼지 여섯 마리의 간을 가져와 다른 여섯 형제의 간이라고 속이고 노일제대귀일의 딸에게 바쳤다. 그녀도 간을 먹을 정도로 괴물은 아니었는지, 자리를 비켜달라고 하고는 먹는 시늉만 한 채 이불 속에 간을 숨겨두었다. 그러나 녹디성인은 이 모든 광경을 지켜보고 있었다. 노일제대귀일의 딸은 막내의 간까지 먹어야 병이 낫겠다고 말했다. 녹디성인은 더 이상 분노를 참을 수 없었다. 이불 밑에서 간을 꺼내 옥상으로 올라가 마을 사람들에게 이 여자가 어떻게 어머니로 변장해 자신과 형제들을 죽이려 했는지 전부 이야기했다. 곧 온 동네에 소문이 퍼졌고, 성이 난 사람들이 집안으로 몰려들었다. 남선비와 노일제대귀일의 딸의 온몸이 흔들릴 정도로 우레와 같은 소리가 났다. 겁에 질린 노일제대귀일의 딸은 스스로 운명을 달리하기로 했다. 집 바깥으로 뛰쳐나가 자기 머리카락으로 목을 맸다. 남선비도 아들들을 죽일 뻔했다는 죄책감에 사로잡혀 공포에 질린 채 뛰쳐나가던 중, 집 앞 정주목에 부딪혀 정낭에 목이 끼어 죽었다. 남선비의 영혼은 그대로 그곳에 갇혀 성문을 수호하는 주목지신이 되었다.

    남선비의 형체는 사라졌지만, 정주목의 정낭으로 의

사표현을 할 수 있었다. 정주목의 구멍은 남선비의 입, 정낭은 남선비의 이빨이 되었다. 정낭 배치를 통해 다음 네 가지의 상황을 알릴 수 있다.[63]

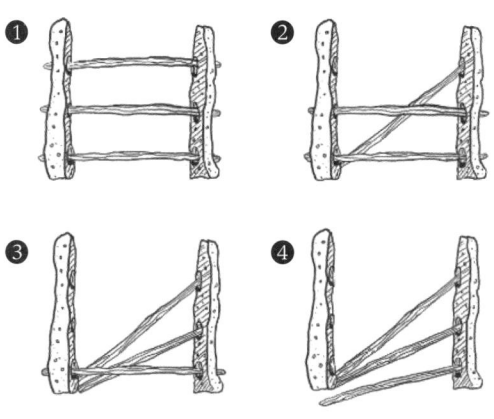

❶ 세 구멍을 정낭으로 전부 끼워 넣으면 주인이 하루 종일 외출한다는 뜻이다.

❷ 아래 두 정낭만 끼워 넣으면 반나절 정도 자리를 비운다는 뜻이다.

❸ 맨 밑에 정낭만 끼워 넣으면 잠깐 이웃집에 갔다가 금방 돌아온다는 뜻이다.

❹ 정낭을 끼우지 않으면 주인이 집에 있다는 뜻이다.

정주목과 정낭

정낭의 '정'은 제주 방언으로 '잠그다', '낭'은 '나무'를 뜻한다. 정주목의 '주목'은 기둥을 뜻하는 제주 방언 '주먹'에서 왔다.

노일제대귀일의 딸이 스스로 목숨을 끊었으니, 일곱 형제의 복수는 성공한 셈이다. 그러나 노일제대귀일의 딸이 어머니를 죽였을 것이라고 생각한 아들들은 한 번 더 복수를 하기로 결심했다. 그들은 노일제대귀일의 딸 시체의 다리를 절단하여, 그 자리에 뒷간 바닥의 석판을 떼다 붙였다. 시체의 머리는 잘라 돼지 여물통으로 쓰고, 다른 부위들은 잘라 바다에 던졌다. 머리털은 해초가 되었고, 입은 작은 정어리 같은 물고기인 솔치로 변했다. 손톱, 발톱은 따개비가 되었고, 항문은 여러 종류의 조개가 되었다. 노일제대귀일의 딸의 시체는 자연물로 은유 되었다. 시체의 잔해는 바람에 의해 닳아 없어지고, 각다귀와 모기떼로 변했다. 그녀는 끔찍한 모습의 가신이 되었다. 노일제대귀일의 딸은 뒷간 여신, 측도부인(통시할망)이 되었다.

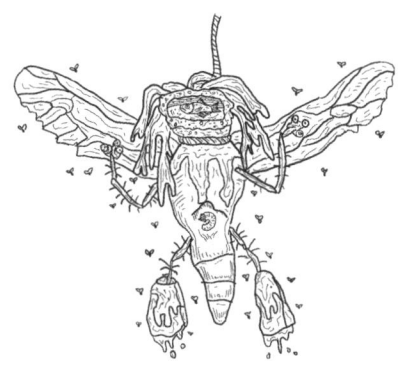

노일제대귀일의 딸

복수를 마친 일곱 형제는 어머니를 되살리기 위해 여정을 떠났다. 그들의 첫 번째 목적지는 윤회의 꽃들을 딸 수 있는 '서천꽃밭'이었다. 서천꽃밭에서 꽃을 딴 후 어머니를 찾아나섰다. 하늘님에게 어머니가 빠져 죽은 주천강의 물을 말려달라고 기도했다. 연못이 바닥을 드러내자 어머니의 유해가 나타났다. 일곱 형제가 유해 위에 꽃을 뿌리자, 조금 전까지 해골이었던 어머니의 몸에 살과 피가 되살아나기 시작했다.

정지(부엌)

일곱 형제는 어머니를 일으켜 세우고 따뜻하게 감싸안았다. 차디찬 호수 아래서 일 년을 지냈지만, 이제는 부엌(제주 방언으로 '정지')의 여신인 조왕할망이 되어, 부뚜막의 따뜻함을 영원히 누릴 수 있을 것이라며 안심시켰다.

조왕할망이 사이가 나쁜 뒷간의 신 측도부인과 가장 멀리 떨어져 있는 주방의 여신이 된 것은 자연스럽다. 제주에는 '통시(뒷간)와 조왕(정지)은 멀수록 좋다'라는 속담이 있다. 뒷간은 주방에서 멀수록 좋다는 말이다. 이것은 위생 측면에서의 은유이기도 하다.[64] '통시'란 제주에서만 볼 수

조왕할망

있는 독특한 형태의 뒷간이다. 제주에서는 변소에 흑돼지를 두어 사람의 배설물을 먹이로 활용하였다. 그래서 노일제대귀일의 딸을 통시할망이라고 부르기도 한다.[65]

남선비의 두 아내의 갈등은 제주 여성들이라면 너무나도 공감할 사연이다. 앞서 이야기했듯이 제주는 바위, 바람, 여자가 많아 하여 '삼다섬'이라 불린다. 바위와 바람이 제주의 풍토와 기후의 산물이라면, 여자는 불행한 역사의 결과다. 남자들이 바다낚시나 강제 노역으로 너무 많이 죽었기 때문이다. 어떤 기록에는 여성이 남성보다 두 배나 인구수가 많았다고 기록되어 있다. 이런 이유로 아내가 여러 명인 남편이 많았다. 조선 후기의 제주 목사를 지냈던 관리의 말에 따르면, 제주에서는 아주 허약한 남자들도 두세 명의 부인을 거느리고 있었고, 많게는 십여 명까지 있었다.[66] 문전 본풀이는 일곱 형제가 신으로 승천하며 끝맺는다. 형제신들은 각각 제주 전통 가옥의 여러 문을 지키는 수호신이 되었다. 그중 영리했던 막내는 상방(마루방)의 앞쪽 대문을 지키는 수호신 '문전신'이 되었다.[67]

상방

문전신

    제주의 전통적인 집은 무덤만큼이나 잘 보호되고 있다. 그만큼 제주의 집과 무덤을 위협하는 요소가 많다는 뜻이기도 한데, 그 중 하나가 바로 식물의 침입이다. 조선시대에는 초목이 집과 너무 가깝게 자라면 집주인에게 큰 불행이 닥친다고 믿었다. 심술궂은 요괴들이 나무에 붙어 침입한다고 생각했다. 이 중에는 '독각'이라고 불리는 한 발로 깡충 뛰는 음탕한 영혼이 있었다. 독각은 집안의 여자를 유혹하고, 거절당하면 밭에 나무로 된 말뚝을 박아 복수했다. 말뚝이 주변 지역을 훼손하여 농작물을 못 자라게 했다.[68]

집안에서 자라는 나무는 더더욱 불길했다. 이러한 생각은 한자에서 비롯된 단어에서도 발견된다. 빈곤(貧困), 피곤(疲困), 곤경(困境), 곤란(困難)에는 모두 '곤(困)'자가 들어간다. 입 구(口) 안에 나무 목(木)이 들어가 있다.[69] 나무가 집안에서 지나치게 무성히 흉흉한 집, 즉 흉가라 여겼다.

흉가

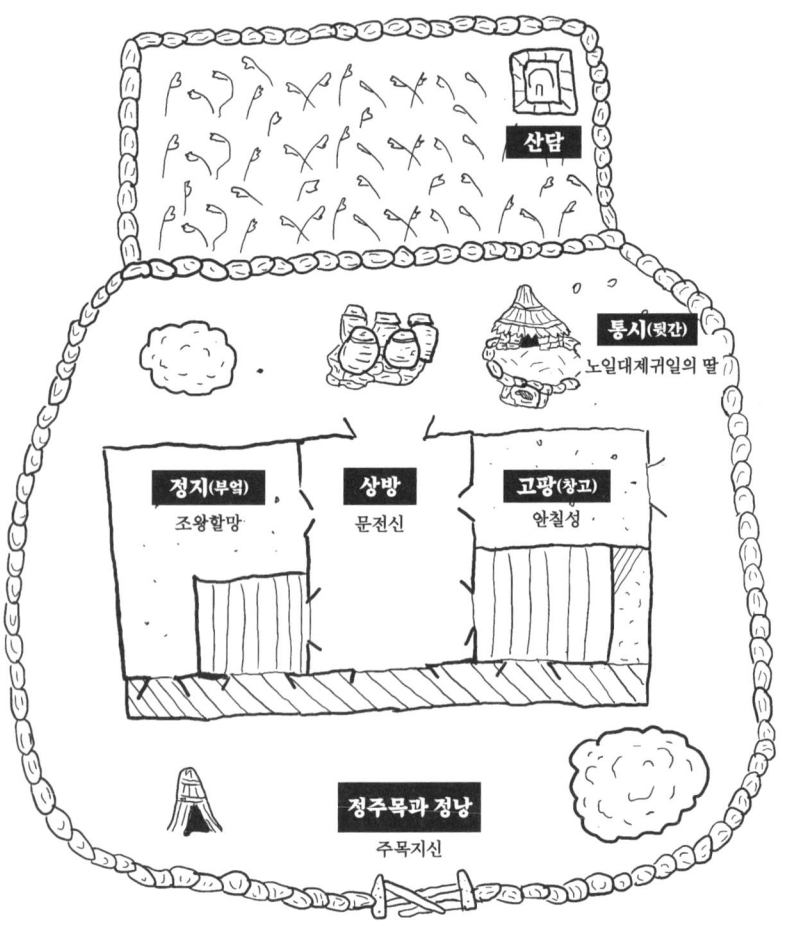

6장.
죽음의 신 카드

~~~~~~~~~~

사만이 조상의 해골

강림

과양생이 부부

사만이 조상의 해골

집안에 기거하는 또 다른 신으로 '조상신'이 있다. 조상신 중에 가장 관대한 신은 아마 '명감본풀이(멩감본풀이)'에 나오는 '사만이' 조상신일 것이다. 사만이는 가족들을 무척 사랑했지만 부양할 능력이 부족했다. 사냥을 나가면 사슴 한 마리 잡지 못했다. 그가 발견한 것이라고는 어느 해골 하나 뿐이었다. 발견했다기보다는 해골이 그를 쫓아왔다고 봐야 맞을 것이다. 아무리 도망을 가도 한 발짝 내디딜 때마다 해골이 그의 앞에 나타났다. 그는 단순한 우연이 아니라고 직감했다. 사만이는 문득 이 해골이 집안을 지켜줄 조상의 해골일 수도 있겠다는 생각이 들었고, 집으로 가져와 고팡의 큰 독 속에 모셨다. 그날 이후로 제사를 지낼 때마다 부모의 위패보다 먼저 해골에 음식을 바쳤다. 공양이 헛되진 않았는지 그의 운명이 점차 바뀌기 시작했다. 사냥을 나가면 사슴 여러 마리를 잡았다. 마을에서 가장 가난했던 사만이는 어느새 큰 부자가 되었다.

모든 일이 순조로운 듯했지만, 사실 사만이에게는 더 큰 위협이 엄습해 오고 있었다. 어느 날 밤, 부인과 함께 잠이 들었는데 고팡에서 백발노인이 나타나 사만이 부부를 깨웠다. 노인은 염라대왕이 저승에서 삼차사를 보내 사만이를 잡아 오라고 명했다고 경고하며, 위협을 피할 길도 알려주었다. 집 앞 삼거리로 나가 병풍을 두르고, 음식을 가득 차려 제사를 올리라고 했다. 상 밑에는 사만이의 이름을 적어 붙여놓고, 차사가 이름을 보고 부르면 대답하라고 했다. 사만이 부부는 노인이 시키는 대로 상을 차렸다. 잠시 후 차사들이 나타났다. 상을 보자마자 자리에 앉아 음식을 먹었다. 다 먹었을 때쯤 상 밑에 적힌 사만이라는 이름을 발견했다. 차사들은 곤혹스러워졌다. 그들이 저승으로 데려가야 할 사람의 이름이었던 것이다. 남의 음식을 공짜로 먹는 일은 교수형에도 처할 수 있는 큰 죄였다. 차사들은 이 음식이 정말 사만이의 것인지 확인하기 위해 사만이의 이름을 불렀고, 사만이는 대답했다. 차사들은 어찌할 바를 몰랐다. 사만이의 집으로 가보니 그곳에는 더 많은 음식이 차려져 있었다. 차사들은 죄책감에 시달리면서도 놀라운 환대에 감동했다. 공짜 음식을 먹었으니 차마 사만이의 목숨을 빼앗을 수 없게 된 차사들은 저승으로 돌아가 동자판관실(이 세상 모든 생명의 수명을 기록해놓은 곳)으로 몰래 잠입했다. 무수한 두루마리 중에 사만이의 기록을 발견했다. 사만이의 수명은 삼십 년으로 정해져 있었다. 차사들은 붓을 들어 한 금을 비껴 그어 '삼십(三十)'을 '삼천(三千)'으로 바꾸었다. 나중에 염라가 돌아와 사만이가 왜 아직 살아있는지 묻자, 차사들은 고친 기록을 보여주었고 염라는 자기가 착각했나보다 생각했다. 그리하여 사만이는 조상의 해골에게 친절한 공덕으로 삼천세까지 살 수 있었다.[70, 71]

명감본풀이가 이승에 사는 우리한테 귀중한 조언을 해준다면, '차사본풀이'는 저승으로 가면 어떤 일이 벌어지는지를 알려준다. 저승차사 중 유명한 이로 '강림'이 있다. 저승차사 강림도 한때는 사만이처럼 고생을 했다. 하급 관리였던 강림은 무리한 임무를 맡았다.

'과양생이 부부'의 세 아들이 한꺼번에 죽은 사건이 일어

강림

났다. 멀쩡히 건강하던 아이들이 갑자기 죽은 일이었다. 고을의 '김치원님'은 강림에게 사건의 진상을 아는 저승의 염라대왕을 데려오라고 했다. 강림의 현명한 부인은 남편의 임무를 듣자마자 필요한 물건들을 준비하였는데, 그 중 하나가 그 집의 조왕할망과 문전신에게 바쳤던 시루떡이었다. 조왕할망과 문전신은 보답으로 강림을 저승으로 인도해 주었다.

그러나 염라를 이승으로 오게 하는 일은 강림이 해내야 할 몫이었다. 강림은 대담하게도 매복을 감행했다. 저승 문 옆에서 기다리다가 염라의 가마가 지나가는 것을 보고 천둥같이 포효하며 돌진했다. 염라의 호위대들이 막을 새도 없이 가마의 가림천을 찢고 들어갔다. 그 안에서 염라는 덜덜 떨고 있었다. 강림은 염라가 숨도 못 쉴 정도로 밧줄로 단단히 결박했다. 염라는 강림이 원하는 것은 무엇이든 들어줄 수밖에 없었다. 김치원님과 과양생이 부부 앞에 나타나 세 아들의 죽음에 얽힌 미스터리를 풀기 시작했다. 염라는 아들들이 죽은 것이 이번이 처음이 아니라고 했다. 처음 그들을 죽인 사람은 과양생이 부부 자신들이었다.

오래전 세 명의 소년이 음식과 잠자리를 구하러 과양생이 부부 집에 찾아왔을 때 첫 번째 죽임을 당했다. 소년들의 시체를 연못에 버렸는데 그곳에서 아름다운 꽃 세 송이가 자랐다. 과양생이의 부인은 실수로 꽃 세 송이를 삼켰고 얼마 뒤 임신했다. 그 뒤로 부인은 세쌍둥이를 얻었고,

과양생이 부부

인생 최대의 행복을 느꼈다. 그러나 어머니의 사랑이 아들들의 운명에 치명적인 독이 될 줄은 전혀 몰랐다. 과양생이의 세 아들은 과거시험에서 장원급제하여 돌아오자마자 목이 꺾여 죽었다.

염라는 과양생이 부부가 느낀 고통이 충분하지 않다고 생각하여 부부를 가장 끔찍한 방법으로 죽이라고 명했다. 부부는 각각 다른 방향으로 달리는 아홉 마리의 소에 묶여 사지가 찢겨 죽었다. 그러나 그것으로도 염라는 성에 차지 않았다. 그들이 저지른 죄를 벌하려면 그 존재를 완전히 없애버려도 모자랄 것이었다. 염라는 힘 좋은 젊은 여자들을 방앗간에 불러들여 찢어지고 남은 유골을 방아에 넣어 고운 가루로 부수게 했다. 후하고 가루를 불었더니 모기와 각다귀로 환생하여 사방으로 날아갔다.

염라는 인간에 불과한 몸으로 세상을 여행하며 큰 용기를 보여준 강림에게 크게 감명받아 김치원님에게 강림을 달라고 요청했다. 김치원님이 이를 거절하자 늙은 염라는 꾀를 내어 타협안을 제시했다. 강림의 육신은 김치원님이 갖고, 강림의 영혼은 염라가 가져가겠다는 것이다. 어리석은 김치원님은 염라의 제안을 수락했다. 강림은 가엾게도 자기 의견은 말하지도 못했다. 그대로 육신에서 빠져나온 강림의 영혼은 저승으로 끌려갔고, 죽은 자의 영혼을 저승으로 안내하는 저승사자가 되었다. 한편 자신이 유리한 거래를 했다고 믿었던 김치원님은 강림의 육신에게 이것저것 명령하기 시작했다. 하지만 그 명령이 강림의 귀에 들릴리 없었다. 영혼 없는 육신은 죽은 것과 다름없기 때문이다.[72]

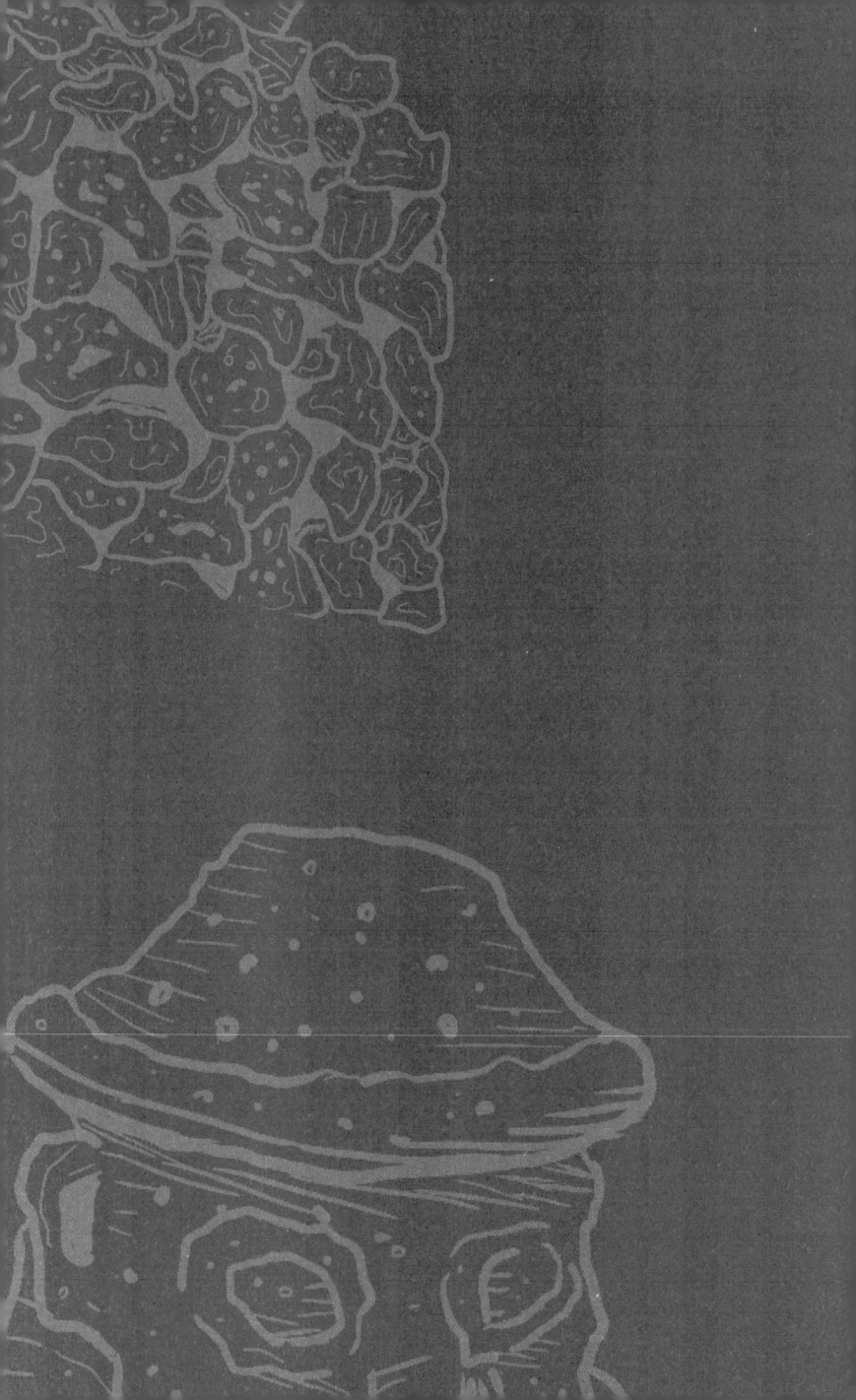

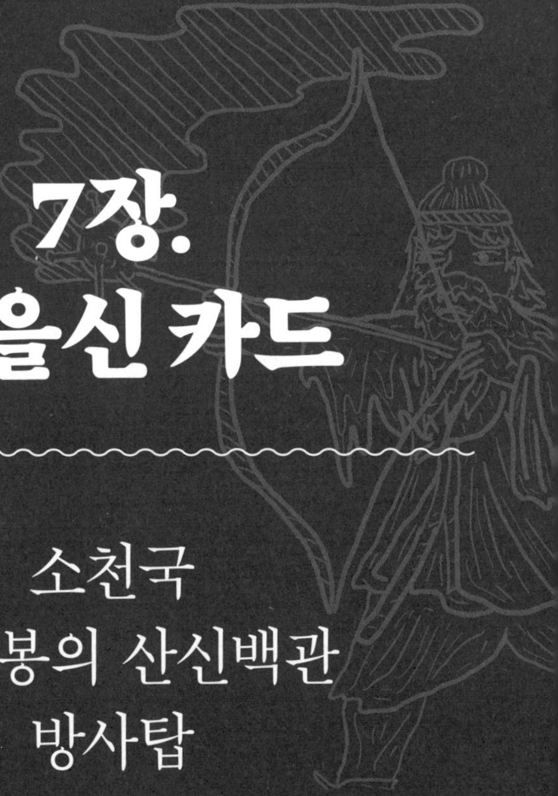

7장.
마을신 카드

소천국
고내봉의 산신백관
방사탑
돌하르방

소천국

제주에는 각 마을을 지키는 수호신인 본향당신이 있다. 한때 마을의 조상이었다가 신이 된 존재들로,[73] 후손들의 삶과 죽음, 생계를 관장한다. 본향당은 지역 주민들, 특히 여성들이 아이의 탄생, 가족의 죽음, 한 해의 수확 상태 등의 삶의 중요한 과제들을 논의하는 마을회관과 같은 역할을 했다.[74]

본향당신 이야기 '송당본풀이'를 소개한다. '소천국'과 그의 부인 '백주또'는 딸 28명과 아들 18명을 낳았다. 훗날 소천국과 백주또의 자식들은 각각 마을을 세워 그 마을의 본향당신이 되었다. 다산의 결실을 보았지만, 부부 생활은 행복하지 않았다. 제주의 사냥꾼이었던 소천국과 중국에서 농사꾼으로 살던 백주또는 출신부터 삶의 방식까지 너무 달랐다. 소천국은 백주또를 따라 농사를 지으려고 했지만 뜻대로 잘 되지 않았다. 어느 날 소천국이 정신없이 밭을 갈고 있을 때 지나가던 스님이 소천국의 음식을 다 먹어치웠다. 스님이 그걸 다 먹어치운 것은 퍽 대단한 일이었는데, 왜냐하면 소천국은 식욕이 엄청나서 백주또가 점심으로 챙겨준 양이 어마어마했기 때문이다. 소천국은 점심으로 먹을 아홉 그릇의 밥과 아홉 그릇의 국이 다 없어진 것을 보고는 거의 기절할 뻔했다. 식욕이 왕성한 소천국에게 가장 힘든 일은 배고픔을 참는 것이었다. 당장 뭐라도 먹지 않으면 굶어 죽을 것 같았다. 이 배고픔을 해결해야 했다. 그때 쟁기를 끌던 소가 눈에 들어왔다. 소는 그에게 너무나 소중한 일꾼이었지만 지금 소천국의 눈에는 점심거리로밖에 보이지 않았다. 그는 소를 때려잡아 쇠갈퀴 같은 손톱으로 가죽을 벗겨내어 구웠다. 소 한 마리를 다 먹어도 여전히 배가 고팠다. 이웃 밭에 있는 소까지 잡아먹고 나서야 배가 불렀다.

이 사실을 알게 된 백주또는 믿을 수 없을 정도로 큰 충격에 빠졌다. 남편이 최악의 도둑놈이 된 것이다. 백주또는 그 자리에서 결혼 생활을 끝내자고 했다. 부인의 마음을 돌릴 수 없었던 소천국은 짐을 챙겨 그날로 바로 떠났다. 소천국은 원래 살던 방식으로 돌아가 한라산 중턱 동굴에 새 보금자리를 마련하여 사냥꾼의 삶을 이어갔다. 소천국은 지금도 알손당의 사냥신으로 모셔져 있다.[75]

울창한 숲으로 뒤덮인 한라산은 사냥에 적합했다. 그러나 한라산은 사냥터 이상의 의미를 지니고 있다. 한라산은 섬 어디에서든지 볼 수 있으며, 내륙의 대부분을 차지하고 있어 신들의 고향으로 여겨졌다. 한라산은 '은하수를 끌어내리는 봉우리'라고 하여, 이름에서부터 그 위엄을 느낄 수 있다.[76] 사람들은 제주 사냥 문화에서 수렵신들의 중요성, 그리고 그들의 신성함을 바탕으로 수렵신들이 한라산과 밀접한 관련이 있다고 생각했다. 수렵신을 산의 신이라 믿으며 '산신'이라고 불렀다.

고내봉의 산신백관

그렇다고 제주의 산신들이 모두 한라산에 살고 있는 것은 아니다. 북서쪽 해안의 고내봉 오름에는 '산신백관'이 자리하고 있다. 백관(百官)은 나라의 높은 관직을 가진 여러 관리를 뜻하며 대부분 과거 시험을 통과한 이들이었다. 신들에게 백관이란 칭호를 붙여 위신을 부여한 것이다. '산신백관'은 풍수 등 천문 지리에 능통한 산신에게 붙여졌다. 그러나 백관의 직함을 갖고 있다고 산신들 중에서 가장 명석한 것은 아니었다.

어떤 산신백관은 자신을 모셔줄 사람들을 끌어들이는 방법을 모른 채, 고내봉 꼭대기에 좌정하여 허기진 채 공양물을 기다리기만 했다. 아무도 자신을 찾지 않자 당황한 산신백관은 인간 친구 초립동이를 불러 이유를 물었다. 초립동이는 공양을 받고 싶으면 언덕 위에 앉아 있지만 말고 좀 더 적극적으로 나서야 한다고 말하며, 인근 마을 입구 쪽으로 화살을 쏘아보라고 조언했다. 그러면 질병이 퍼질 테고 불안해진 주민들이 신을 달래야 한다고 생각하게 될 거라는 것이다. 초립동이의 말대로 하자 곧 마을 전체에 전염병이 돌았다. 마을 사람들은 이번에는 무당이 아닌 마을신 송씨할망을 찾아 조언을 구했다. 송씨할망은 산신백관에게 제물을 바치고 고내봉에서 가장 순수하고 양지바른 곳에 그를 위한 신당을 지으라고 조언했다. 시키는 대로 하자 전염병은 곧 가라앉았다. 좋은 위치에 신당이 지어지자 곧 다른 신들도 몰려들기 시작했다. 산신은 충신 초립동

이를 포함한 다른 신들과 함께 신당에 좌정했다.[77]

신이라고 다 자신의 신당이나 기원 이야기가 있지는 않다. 대표적인 예로 '방사탑'이 있다. 방사탑은 단순한 커다란 원형 돌무더기 모양으로 되어 있지만, 제주의 다른 어느 신당보다 훨씬 눈에 잘 띈다.

'방사탑'의 '防(방)'은 '막다', '邪(사)'는 '악'을 뜻한다. 즉 사악함을 막는 탑이다. 제주의 어떤 안내판에는 '악을 쫓아내는 탑'이라고 번역되어 있는데, 이 설명이 더 적절한 것 같다.[78] 방사탑의 다른 이름으로는 답, 답단이, 거욱, 거왁, 거옥대 등이 있다.[79] 방사탑을 배치할 때도 풍수지리를 중요하게 고려하였는데 집 쪽으로 부는 무시무시한 바람을 조금이라도 막는 것이 중요했다. 제주 사람들은 해풍을 막기 위해 돌담을 쌓거나 집 주변에 나무를 심었다.[80] 그러나 이러한 방법들은 너무 돈이 많이 들고 시간도 오래 걸렸다. 방사탑을 세우는 것이 경제적으로 더 좋은 방법이었다. 방사탑은 마을에서 가장 잘 보이는 곳에 세웠다. 대표적인 예로 제주 남서부 인성리 대정성 마을의 방사탑이 있다. 남쪽으로 알뱅디 평지가 있는데, 예로부터 마을 농가를 황폐하게 만드는 화재의 근원지였다. 이 화재는 네 개의 방사탑을 세운 후에야 끝이 났다고 한다. 그중 세 개는 오늘날까지 남아있다. 세 개의 탑은 단순한 돌무더기가 아니다. 탑 위에 새를 닮은 바위나 작은 돌하르방 돌멩이를 설치해 마을을 지키게 했다.

제주의 여러 신 중에서 한국인들이 가장 좋아하는 신은 '돌하르방'이다. 불룩하게 튀어나온 동공 없는 눈, 넓은 코, 버섯모양 모자를 쓰고 희미한 미소를 머금은 친근하고 다정한 모습이다. 큰 이목구비 때문에 다소 우스꽝스러워 보일 수 있지만, 항상 두 손으로 가슴을 꽉 움켜쥔 채 꼿꼿이 서 있는 모습에서 위엄과 강인함을 느낄 수 있다. 돌하르방은 돌로 만들어졌지만, 이것은

돌하르방

그냥 돌이 아니다. 돌하르방의 몸은 섬 전역에 있는 현무암으로 만들어졌다. 움푹 팬 자국이 있는 것이 특징이다. 지금의 돌하르방은 관광 홍보대사가 되었지만, 이전에는 방사탑과 함께 제주의 '수호신'으로 불렸다. 알뱅디 방사탑처럼 돌하르방도 때때로 넷씩 무리를 지은 채 세워져 있다. 대정현성과 성읍리 대문 앞에는 옛 돌담의 위용을 그대로 간직한 돌하르방이 침입자를 경계하며 경비를 서고 있다.

돌하르방은 보초 역할만 하는 게 아니다. 그들은 다산을 부르는 힘이 있었다. 그 이유를 알기 위해서는 돌하르방의 외모를 다시 살펴볼 필요가 있다. 돌하르방이 쓰고 있는 버섯 모양 모자는 조선시대 남자들이 많이 썼던 벙거지를 모방한 것으로 추정된다. 모자를 뒤쪽과 옆에서 보았을 때 남근을 닮았다고 하여 양기를 상징하게 되었다. 돌하르방의 형태에서 다산을 상징하는 또다른 부분은 코다. 한국에서는 돌하르방처럼 튀어나온 코가 정력을 상징한다고 봤다. '장모는 좋겠네 장인 코가 커서'라는 말이 그래서 나온 것이다. 제주 여성들은 다산의 기운을 받고자 돌하르방의 코를 쓰다듬었고, 한밤중에 몰래 돌하르방 돌조각을 긁어내 물에 섞어 마셨다고 한다.[81] 그런데 돌하르방이 제주에 생긴 지는 그리 오래되지 않았다.

《탐라기년》에 의하면 1754년 제주 목사 김몽규가 성문 밖에 '옹중석'을 세웠다고 한다.[82] 돌하르방이라고 불리게 된 것은 비교적 최근 일이다. 돌하르방은 동북아시아 전역의 다른 조각상들과 연관 지어 설명하기도 한다. 육지의 장승 조각상들이 기원이라는 이야기, 중국 진시황 때 세운 장수 안옹중의 동상이 옹중석의 시초였다는 이야기[83], 몽골의 '하라바라칸(망보는 물체)' 조각상들이 기원이라는 이야기 등이 있다.[84]

8장.
제주 수호신과 공격신 카드

김통정

광양당신

산호 해녀

장길손

김통정

외지에서 온 모든 신이 돌하르방처럼 따뜻하게 환영받기만 한 것은 아니었다. 돌하르방은 섬사람들을 보호하고 풍요롭게 만들어 주었지만 어떤 신은 죽음과 파괴를 불러들였다.

고려시대 삼별초를 이끌었던 김통정 장군이 대표적이다. 삼별초는 1270년 고려왕이 몽골에 항복하자 이에 대항하여 반란을 일으킨 군대다. 서남쪽에 위치한 진도를 근거지로한 삼별초는 반도 전역을 급습했으나 고려군과 몽골 연합군에 맞서 싸우다 1271년 쫓겨났다.

삼별초 장수 중 배중손은 전사했지만, 김통정은 살아

남았다. 남은 병력을 이끌고 겨우 탈출에 성공한 김통정은 제주로 후퇴하여 최후의 항전을 준비했다. 그러나 1273년 고려-몽골 연합군이 제주에 침입하면서 삼별초는 전멸되었고 김통정은 살해당했다. 하지만 삼별초의 저항 정신은 계속 이어졌고, 김통정 장군은 전설의 인물이 되었다.[85]

김통정은 육지에서는 순교자로 기억되지만, 제주의 많은 전설 속에서는 악당으로 그려진다. 김통정은 제주에 도착하자마자 주민들을 억압했다고 한다. 방어 시설을 구축하기 위해 주민들을 징집했는데, 지금도 애월읍 일대에 그 토성이 남아 있다. 거대한 토성을 쌓기 위해 주민들을 노예처럼 부렸으며, 성벽이 완성되고는 아무런 보상을 하지 않았다고 한다. 또한 병사들을 시켜 주민들의 귀중한 농작물을 빼앗아 새로 만든 요새에 두었다. 들판에 농작물을 남겨두긴 했지만 주민들은 이미 지칠 대로 지쳐 그마저도 거둘 수 없었고, 농작물들은 그렇게 밭에서 썩어 갔다.[86] 그러나 김통정은 이러한 고통을 보고도 멈추지 않았다. 그는 병사들을 시켜 성벽 꼭대기에 재를 뿌리게 하고 말 꼬리에 빗자루를 매달아 채찍을 내리쳤다. 말이 토성 위를 달리자, 재가 공중으로 흩뿌려지면서 천지 분간이 어려워졌다. 그의 요새는 난공불락 같았다. 어떤 적이 나타나도 검은 재에 휩싸여 길을 잃었을 것이었다. 김통정의 최후의 방어책은 불행하게도 또 다른 적을 만들었다. 그들은 '광양당신'과 두 동생들로, '광양당 본풀이'에 의하면 이들은 백주또와 소천국의 아들이라고 한다.[87] 광양당신은 셋 중 가장 강력한 힘을 지니고 있었다.

어둠이 찾아오자 광양당신 삼형제는 행동에 나섰다. 김통정은 이상한 낌새를 눈치챘지만, 자신의 힘으로 방어할 수 없는 상대라는 것을 직감하고 탈출을 감행했다. 김통정도 평범한 사람은 아니어서, 요술을 부려 만든 무쇠방석을 타고 빠르게 도망쳤다. 하지만 이게 끝이 아니었다. 김통정은 바다 위를 떠다니다 또 다른 적과 마주했다. 바다의 용왕들은 김통정이 탄 무쇠 방석을 물속으로 끌어내렸다. 그는 결국 무쇠 방석을 버리고 간신히 용왕들의 손아귀에서 벗어난 뒤 매로 변신하여 날아갔다. 그러나 김통정은 광양당신 형제들도 변신할 것이라고 예상하지 못했다. 광양당신 형제들은 두 마리의 새와 한 마리의 모기가 되어 맹렬히 추격하여 뒤를 바짝 따라잡았다. 그때가 되어서야 김통정의 귀에 우레와 같은 날갯

광양당신

짓 소리, 윙윙거리는 모기 소리가 들렸다. 김통정은 무쇠 비늘을 둘러 방어를 단단히 한 상태였지만, 뒤를 돌아보려고 고개를 돌린 순간 목을 감싸고 있던 단단한 비늘 갑옷이 들리며 단 하나의 약점이 드러났다. 광양당신은 그 틈을 노려 비수를 꽂았다. 김통정은 단번에 숨을 거두었고, 그의 피는 파도에 흩뿌려졌다.[88]

    광양당신에 의해 수장된 침략자가 또 한 명 있었다. 그는 중국인 지관 '고종달이(호종단)'였다. 풍수지리를 통해 제주의 힘을 악화시키고자 중국에서 파견한 인물이었다. 풍수지리는 땅 밑을 흐르는 기운이 인간의 운명에 영향을 미친다는 믿음에서 비롯된다. 고종달이는 이웃나라에 제왕감이 태어나지 못하도록 그 기운을 끊어내는 임무를 맡았다. 처음에는 매우 성공적이었다. 고종달이는 산방산 일대를 샅샅이 돌며, 맥을 끊기에 가장 요긴한 '용머리' 바위를 찾았다. 용의 꼬리와 잔등 부분을 끊자마자 바위에서 피가 철철 흘러나와 주변 바다로 흘러갔고, 고통에 찬 신음소리가 산방산을 울렸다. 지금도 용머리 해안 절벽에는 기괴한 무늬가 남아있는데, 묘하게 용이 절단된 자리와 흡사하다. 이렇게 제주의 풍경은 영원한 상처를 품고 있다.[89]

그러나 고종달이는 여기서 멈추지 않았다. 고향으로 돌아가기 전 마지막으로 차귀도로 향했다. 땅이 분노하였는지 고종달이에게 갑자기 매 한 마리가 날아들었다. 처음에는 별로 신경 쓰지 않았는데, 가까이 다가가서 보니 바다를 휘젓고 있었다. 서서히 해일이 그림자를 드리우며 불어닥쳤다. 고종달이는 파도를 피할 수 없었다. 매가 머리 위를 날아가는 순간, 파도가 들이닥치며 배를 산산조각 냈다. 고종달이와 선원들은 거센 파도에 휩쓸려 바다에 빠져 죽었다. 주위를 맴돌던 매는 만족스러운 표정을 지으며 그들의 모습을 내려다보았다. 그는 과연 제주의 적들을 물리치고 다시 한번 승리한 '광양당신'이었다.

그러나 광양당신도 정복하지 못한 단 하나의 적이 있었으니, 천연두의 신 마마신이다. '마마'는 천연두를 뜻하며, 많은 사람들이 두려워하였다.[90] 먼 옛날 마마신은 일 년에 한 번씩 제주에 방문했다고 한다. 결코 환영받는 존재는 아니었지만, 섬사람들은 봄과 가을 사이에 마마신이 올 것을 대비했다. 해마다 호화로운 잔치를 열어 마마신을 맞이했고, 마마신은 만족스럽게 떠나며 섬사람들을 죽이지 않았다. 그러던 어느 해, 마마신은 차린 음식이 충분하지 않다며 불평하며 전 지역에 천연두를 퍼뜨리기 시작했다. 주민들이 아무리 피해 다녀도 병이 따라다녔다. 거대한 돌담도 쌓아보고 동굴에 숨어보려고도 했지만 모두 헛수고였다. 그렇다고 희망이 완전히 사라진 것은 아니었다. 사람들은 마마신을 쫓아낼 방법을 생각했다. '동해용궁'에는 천연두를 퇴치하는 특별한 산호가 자라고 있었다. 그러나 산호를 채취하는 일은 무척 위험천만하여 아무도 그 길을 선뜻 나서지 못했다. 그런데 남쪽의 모슬포 항구에서 갓 잠수일을 시작한 소녀 한 명이 나섰다. '잠수'는 해녀의 원래 명칭이다. 소녀는 이제 막 수영을 배우고 훈련을 시작한 경험이 거의 없는 '애기잠수'였다. 애기잠수는 초보 해녀를 뜻한다.[91]

애기잠수는 경험은 부족할지언정 결단력이 대단했다. 차가운 바다에 뛰어들어 동해용궁까지 헤엄쳐 갔다. 끝이 보이지 않는 넓고 깊은 바다보다 더 난감했던 건 동해용왕이었다. 잠수가 아무리 애원하여도, 용왕은 신성한 산호

산호 해녀

를 내주지 않았다. 산호는 이곳에만 있는 귀중한 보물이기 때문에 절대 용궁 밖으로 가져갈 수 없다는 것이었다. 하지만 용왕은 섬 주민들에게 완전히 무관심하지는 않아서, 산호 대신 마마신을 무찌를 강력한 군대를 파견해 주었다. 용왕의 군대는 뭍으로 올라오는 길에 바위신령의 군사와 연합했다. 막강한 군단을 이끌고 돌아오자 섬 주민들은 드디어 우리가 살 수 있게 되었다며 기뻐했다. 그러나 이것은 불행하게도 착각에 불과했다. 바위신령과 용왕 군대 연합군도 마마신의 맹공격을 버텨낼 수 없었다. 곧 그들의 시체들이 땅 위에 널브러졌다. 지금도 바위신령의 차가운 시신은 마마신 병사들이 쏜 창과 화살에 맞아 구멍 난 돌의 모습으로 남아 있다. 그런데 실의에 빠진 섬사람들 앞에 또 한 번의 충격적인 사건이 일어났다. 용감한 소녀, 애기잠수의 시신이 밀물과 함께 해안으로 떠밀려온 것이다. 애기잠수의 시신에 다가갔더니 놀라운 변화가 일어났다. 오색광채가 연기처럼 애기잠수 위에 내려앉았고, 안개가 걷히자 잠수의 모습은 사라지고 동해용궁의 산호가 빛나고 있었다. 애기잠수의 희생으로 섬사람들은 마침내 마마신을 해안에서 몰아냈다.[92] 마을 사람들을 구한 건 신이 아니라 산호해녀가 된 애기잠수였다.

장길손

제주 신화의 또 다른 영웅, 거인 '장길손' 이야기는 여러 버전으로 변형되어 구전되고 있다. 공통적으로 온순한 거인으로 묘사되나 알고 보면 코믹하면서도 불쌍한 인물이다. 온 땅을 누비던 장길손은 한걸음에 강과 숲을 건널 정도로 덩치가 컸다. 그러나 큰 키는 오히려 약점이었다. 어떤 음식도 그의 비대한 배를 채울 수 없었고, 어떤 옷도 그의 몸을 다 가려주지 못했다. 간신히 중요 부위만 조잡한 나뭇잎으로 덮어 보호할 수 있었다. 장길손은 영원히 굶주린 채

비바람을 맞으며 비참한 모습으로 세상을 떠돌아야 했다.

천하를 전전하던 장길손. 우리나라 남쪽 지방에 도착하면서부터 운명이 바뀌기 시작했다. 사람들이 그를 보고도 도망가거나 숨지 않았다. 귀한 손님 대접하듯 맞이하며, 왕에게나 어울릴법한 잔치를 베풀어 주었다. 장길손은 드디어 배불리 먹을 수 있게 되었다. 사람들의 자비는 여기서 그치지 않았다. 장길손이 입기에도 벅찰 큰 옷을 만들어주었다. 그는 기쁨에 겨워 어쩔 줄 몰랐다. 그런데 이 무슨 잔인한 운명의 장난인지, 주민들의 환대에 감사를 표하려 한 행동이 오히려 그들의 등을 돌리게 했다. 새 옷을 입고 행복해진 장길손은 자리에서 벌떡 일어나 춤을 추기 시작했다. 그런데 그의 춤사위로 그림자가 드리워지면서 햇볕을 가리는 바람에 사람들의 농작물에 피해가 갔다.

결국 북녘으로 쫓겨난 장길손은 다시 굶주리게 되었다. 더 이상 그에게 먹을 것을 줄 사람도 없어졌다. 절망에 빠진 장길손은 흙과 돌들을 주워 먹다가 배탈이 나 위아래로 온갖 배설물이 걷잡을 수 없이 쏟아져나왔다. 그 양이 얼마나 많았으면 지형을 바꿀 정도였다. 장길손의 구토는 한반도 최고봉인 백두산이 되었고, 눈물은 압록강과 두만강이 되었으며, 오줌을 세차게 내갈기자 바다가 되어 한국과 일본이 나뉘게 되었다. 똥은 사방으로 튀어 날아갔는데 그 중 덩어리 하나가 한국 남쪽 바다에 떨어져 제주도가 되었다고 한다.[93]

9장.
다산의 신 카드

삼승할망
구삼승할망
신소미

삼승할망

장길손이 배탈이 나서 엉겁결에 제주를 만들어냈다면 '설문대할망'은 좀 더 장엄한 비전으로 제주를 창조했다. 작지만 모든 것이 조화로운 세상을 만들고자 했다. 중심에는 거대한 산이 있고 가장자리는 평평한 땅을 가진 지상낙원 같은 곳이었다. 어떤 이야기에서는 설문대할망이 제주를 최고의 섬으로 만들기 위해 목숨까지 바쳤다고 한다. 한라산의 아흔 아홉 골짜기에는 설문대할망의 본질이 스며들어 있다. 설문대할망은 물장올 오름 정상에 있는 산정호수로 뛰어들어 자연물과 하나가 되었다. 어머니를 잃은 오백장군은 통곡하여 어머니를 찾아다니다 굳어져 바위가 되었다. 해마다 봄이 되면 물장올 오름에서는 진달래, 철쭉이 무더기로 피어나 한라산을 붉게 물들인다고 한다.[94] 설문대할망은 할머니가 손주 대하듯 섬사람들을 사랑했다. 그래서 제주 방언으로 할머니를 뜻하는 '할망'이라는 이름이 붙었지만, '할망'은 나이에 상관없이 모든 여성 신들을 지칭할 때도 쓰인다.

섬사람들을 무척 사랑했던 또 다른 할망이 있다. 삼승할망은 아이의 잉태를 관장하는 신이다.[95] 육지에서 부르는 다산의 여신 '삼신할머니'를 제주에서는 '삼승할망'이라고 부른다.

삼승할망은 섬사람들에게 생명의 탄생이라는 기적을 내렸다. 능력은 때로 벌로 사용되기도 했다. '마누라 본풀이'는 힘센 마마신 '대별상'을 굴복시키기 위해 '삼승할망'이 자신의 무기를 어떻게 사용했는지 보여준다. 마마신 대별상이 섬 아이들에게 천연두를 퍼뜨려 괴롭히자, 삼승할망은 대별상의 아내, '서신국'을 임신시키고 아이를 낳지 못하게 했다.

'서신국 마누라'의 아기는 출산 예정일이 몇 달이나 지났는데도 나올 생각을 안 했다. 그녀의 몸이 꽃병처럼 부어

올랐다. 견딜 수 없는 고통이 밀려들었고 산모와 아이 둘 다 죽기 일보 직전에 이르렀다. 대별상은 자존심을 굽히고 삼승할망에게 용서를 빌었다. 그러나 삼승할망은 대별상의 사과가 마음에 차지 않았다. 대별상은 참회하는 마음으로 머리를 밀고 승려복을 입었다. 삼승할망은 대별상의 권력을 제한하여, 앞으로 수두에 걸린 아이들만 병에 걸리게 하도록 약속을 받아냈다.

    삼승할망은 심술궂은 '구삼승할망'으로부터도 아이들을 보호했다. 그러나 '구삼승할망'은 대별상보다는 동정심이 많았다. 구삼승할망의 악행은 언제나 실패했다. 구삼승할망은 임신하는 방법에 대해서만 알고 어떻게 출산하는지에 대해서는 아무것도 알지 못했다. 제주의 최고신 천지왕은 그녀를 다른 젊은 여성으로 대체했다. 구삼승할망이 반발하자 천지왕은 모래밭에서 누가 진정한 삼승할망이 될 수 있는지를 가리는 꽃 기르기 시합을 열었다. 천지왕이 내세운 신이 아름다운 꽃밭을 키울 동안, 구삼승할망은 비참한 파멸과 멸망의 꽃들만 피워냈다. 누가 봐도 승부 결과는 의심의 여지가 없었다. 천지왕은 구삼승할망에게 살아있는 아기의 안녕이 아닌 죽은 아기의 영혼을 관장하도록 했다. 구삼승할망은 죽은자들의 땅인 저승으로 내려

가게 되었다.

구삼승할망은 천지왕의 해결책이 전혀 마음에 들지 않았다. 복수를 다짐하며, 상대의 꽃의 잔가지를 잘라내며 이제부터 모든 아이들이 병에 시달리게 될 것이라고 경고했다. 오직 태어나서 백 일을 버틴 아이만 살려둘 것이라고 했다. 천지왕도 구삼승할망의 저주를 풀기엔 역부족이었다. 다행히 새로운 삼승할망이 똑똑하고 능력이 있었다. 새 삼승할망은 구삼승할망에게 타협안을 제시했다. 저주를 거둬들이면 백일을 맞이한 아이의 부모로부터 제물을 받

구삼승할망

을 수 있게 해주겠다는 것이었다. 구삼승할망은 제안을 흡족해하며 받아들이며 천지왕 앞에 엎드렸다. 한 손에는 멸망꽃을 든 채 이승을 떠나 저승으로 향했다.[96] 한편 새 삼승할망은 이승에서 입지를 다졌다. 웅장한 정자를 짓고 시종들과 함께 살았다. 그중에는 '신소미'도 있었다. 열다섯 이전에 세상을 떠나 서천꽃밭에서 꽃을 돌보는 어린 소녀 영혼들을 '신소미'라고 한다.

신소미

갑작스럽게 생을 마감한 신소미에게는 다른 사람의 생명을 돌보는 일이 주어졌다. 이들이 돌보는 꽃들에는 지상에서 살아온 각자의 삶이 반영되어 있다.[97] 불행히도 이승의 설움은 저승까지 이어졌다. 어렸을 때 먹었던 그릇으로 기르는 꽃에 물을 주었다. 부잣집 아이들은 은동이로, 나무바가지로 밥 먹던 가난한 집 아이들은 조잡한 그릇을 사용하여 꽃에 물을 주었다.[98]

10장.
농사의 신 카드

자청비
정수남이 부엉이
서수왕 따님아기

자청비

서천꽃밭에 대해 잘 아는 또 다른 여신 '자청비'가 있다. 자청비는 제주의 여신 중 가장 다재자능하며 입체적인 캐릭터다. 자청비 기원 설화를 담은 '세경본풀이'에서 자청비는 영재, 사냥꾼, 재봉사, 승려, 장군, 헌신적인 아내, 심지어 헌신적인 남편으로도 나온다. 하지만 무엇보다 자청비의 주요한 정체성은 '농사의 여신'이다. '자청비'라는 이름에는 '스스로 비를 청한다'는 뜻이 있다. 그녀가 내리는 비는 땅을 비옥하게 만들어 풍년이 들게 한다. 자청비는 하늘에서 인간 세상으로 오곡[99]을 내리는 '중세경신'으로도 알려져 있다. 세경본풀이는 자청비가 옥황상제의 아들 문도령과 재회하려는 노력에 관한 이야기다. 문도령은 자청비와 결혼하면서 '상세경신'이 되었다. 하늘에서 태어난 문도령은 농사에 중요한 비를 내려주는 존재였다.

자청비와 문도령의 러브 스토리에는 온갖 역경이 있었다. 자청비 집안의 소를 키우던 정이 없는 정수남이라는 자가 있었다. 정수남이는 자청비보다 한참 아래 계층의 노비였는데, 그만 젊은 주인에게 홀딱 반해버렸다. 문도령을 사랑하는 자청비의 마음을 신경 쓰기는커녕 그 마음을 이용하였다. 정수남이는 자청비에게 한라산 중턱에 있는 못에서 문도령이 궁녀들을 거느리고 놀고 있는 걸 보았다고 전했다. 그러나 이것은 자청비를 유인하기 위한 정수남이의 거짓말이었다. 자청비는 총명한 여자였지만, 사랑하는 사람에 관해서는 마음이 약해졌는지 정수남이 말을 믿었다. 정수남이에게 말 두 필을 준비하여, 문도령이 있는 연못으로 데려가 달라고 했다. 뒤늦게 이 모든 것이 거짓말이었다는 것을 깨달았지만, 때는 이미 늦었다.

외진 계곡에는 정수남이와 자청비 둘뿐이었고, 해가 뉘엿뉘엿 지고 있었다. 하지만 자청비가 곤경에 빠져 있을 리 없다. 정수남이의 계획도 탄탄했지만 자청비가 한 수 위였다. 자청비는 때를 엿보며 기다렸다. 자청비는 정수남이에게 고마워하며 그에게 끌리는 척 했다. 정수남이가 자청비를 끌어안으려하자, 자청비는 자신을 정말 원한다면 차가운 밤공기 속에서 기다려 달라고 말했다. 짐승처럼 밖에서 사랑을 나누고 싶지는 않았던 것일까? 자청비는 꾀를 내어 정수남이에게 작은 움막을 만들도록 하고, 벽을 하나 세우기만 하면 구멍을 뚫어 벽을 계속 다시 만들게 했다. 정수남이의 움막 짓기는 밤새 이어졌다. 결국 지쳐서 잠든 정수남이. 자청비는 근처 덤불에서 가시덩굴을 꺾어와 정수남이의 귀를 찔러 다른 쪽 귀로 관통시켰다.

자청비 입장에서는 정당한 살인이었으나 부모는 그렇게 생각하지 않았다. 그들은 이 사실을 알고 경악하여 딸을 집에서 내쫓았다. 결국 자청비는 부모에게 용서를 구하고자 정수남이를 되살릴 부활의 꽃을 찾으러 서천꽃밭으로 가게 되었다.

꽃밭에 들어선 자청비는 정수남이가 살아있는 것을 보고 깜짝 놀랐다. 예전에 알던 정수남이가 아니었다. 인간의 모습은 없어지고 원한을 품은 영혼만 남아 부엉이의 몸으로 환생해 있었다. 충동을 제어하지 못하던 짐승 같은 남자에게 딱 맞는 운명이었다.

부엉이가 된 정수남이는 서천꽃밭의 재앙 그 자체였

다. 그가 울부짖을 때마다 꽃밭의 꽃들은 쪼그라들면서 죽어갔다. 때마침 찾아온 자청비는 어떻게 해야 정수남이를 잡을 수 있을지 잘 알고 있었다. 자청비는 옷을 벗고 누워 부엉이로 변한 정수남이를 유혹하기 시작했다. 음탕한 부엉이가 급습하려는 순간 화살을 쏘아 쓰러뜨렸다. 그렇다고 영원히 죽은 것은 아니었다. 자청비는 정수남이의 해골에 서천꽃밭에서 꺾은 살살이꽃, 피살이꽃, 뼈살이꽃, 도환생꽃을 뿌렸다. 그리고 때죽나무 막대기로 세 번 후려쳤더니 정수남이가 다시 인간 남자의 몸으로 깨어났다. 그는 문도령과 자청비보다 낮은 지위의 '하세경신', 축신(畜神)이 되어 말과 소를 보호했다.

정수남이 부엉이

한편 자청비가 사랑하는 문도령에게는 약혼한 연인이 있었는데, 바로 서수왕의 딸 '서수왕 따님아기'였다. 문도령이 약혼을 파기하자 서수왕 따님아기는 큰 충격에 빠졌다. 막편지(신랑 집에서 신부 집으로 혼인 성사를 알리는 편지)를 돌려받고 화가 치밀었다. 그녀는 막편지를 불태운 재를 물에 타서 마셨다. 그러고는 방문을 닫고 들어가 드러누워 버렸다. 백일이 지나도록 잠겨 있자, 식구들이 문을 따서 들어가 보았더니 이미 죽은 지 한참이 지난 상태였다. 그러나 시신은 없었고, 원한에 사로잡힌 네 마리의 새로 변해 있었다.

- ◆ 머리에서 두통새가 나왔다.
- ◆ 눈에서 훌깃새가 나왔다.
- ◆ 코에서 악숨새가 나왔다.
- ◆ 입에서 부부간 이간질새가 나왔다.

네 마리의 새는 오늘날에도 부부간의 정을 이간질하고 있다. 그래서 혼례를 올리는 신혼부부들은 서수왕 따님아기를 대접하며 백년해로를 빌었다.[100]

정수남이와 서수왕 따님아기 둘 다 새로 변신했다는 점이 인상 깊다. 여러 문화권에서 죽은 몸에서 빠져나와 날아오른 영혼을 새로 형상화하는 경우가 많았다. 제주에서는 나쁜 기운을 의미하는 '사(邪)'를 '새'라고도 발음한다. 날아다니는 '새'와 '나쁜 기운'의 의미가 둘 다 있는 것이다.[101]

서수왕 따님아기

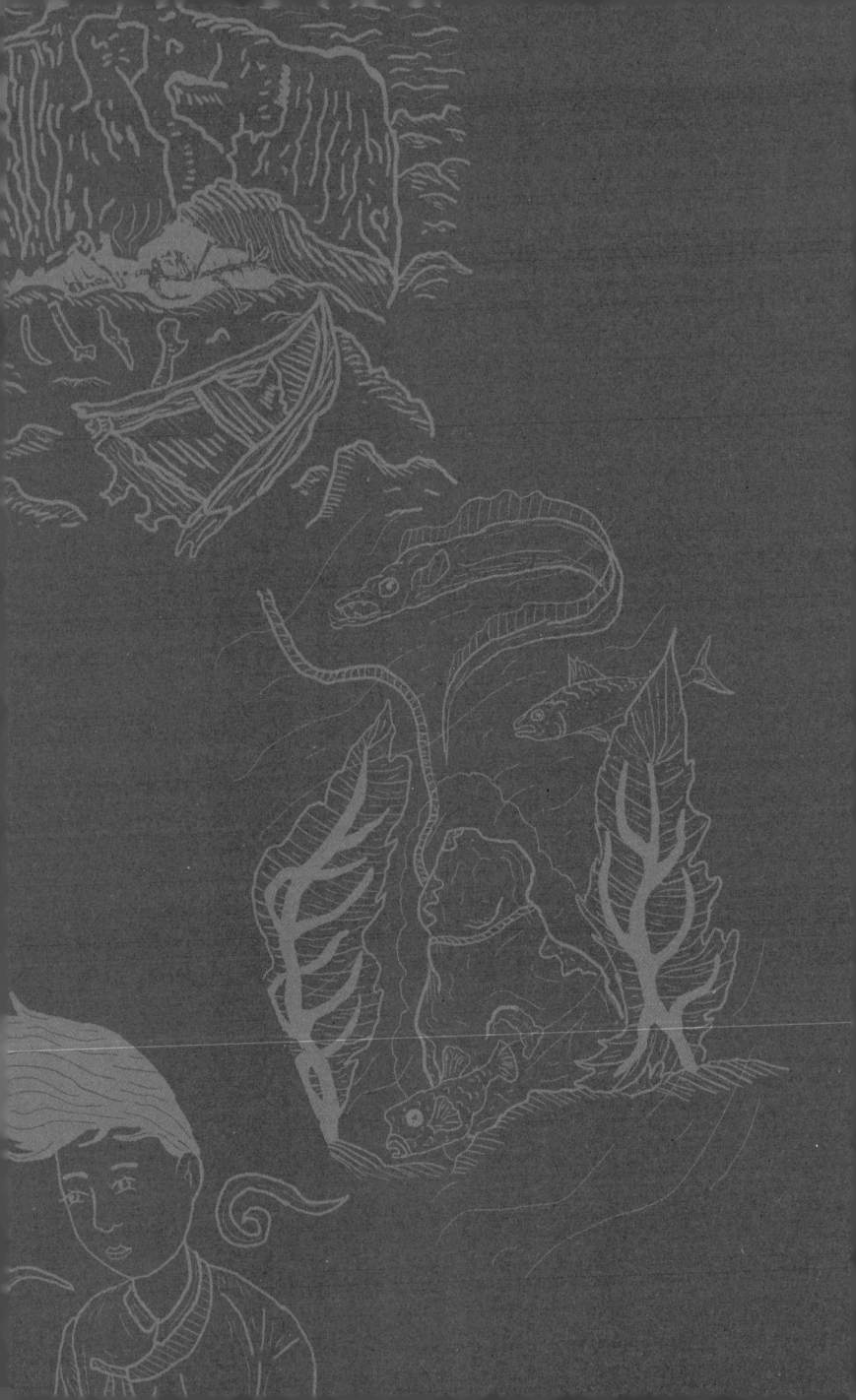

11장.
바다의 신 카드

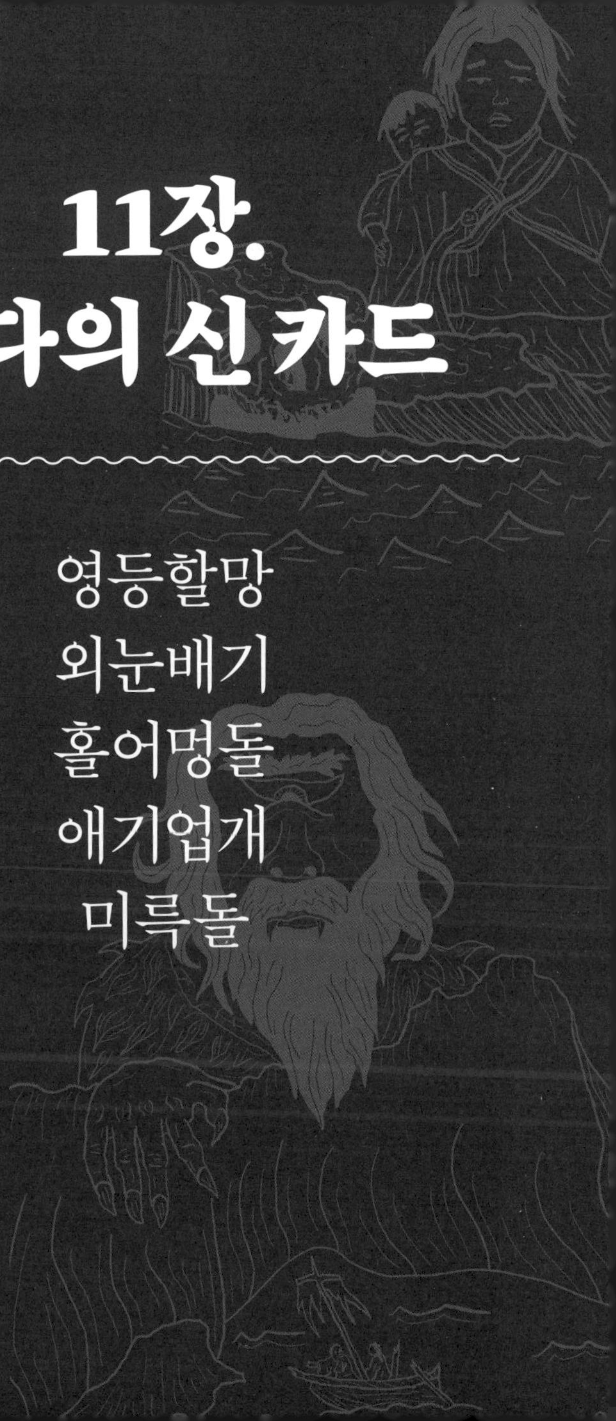

영등할망
외눈배기
홀어멍돌
애기업개
미륵돌

영등할망

삼재(三災)의 섬에서 농사짓는 제주 농부들은 생계를 꾸리기 어려울 때가 많았다. 자청비, 백주또 같은 신들에게 당연히 기댈 수밖에 없었다. 제주 사람들에게 바다만큼 변덕스럽고 예측 불가한 것은 없었기에 해녀와 어부들은 바다신들을 특히 많이 의지하였다.

그중 바람의 신 '영등신'이 있다. 바람을 관장하는 영등신은 다양한 모습으로 나타났다. 왕이나 관리, 때로는 남자, 여자의 모습으로 나타났다. 그중 가장 유명한 신은 '영등할망'이다. 김순이가 기록한 '영등본풀이'의 변형 이야기에서 영등할망은 바다에 사는 아름다운 젊은 여인으로 그려진다.

영등할망에게 바다는 외로운 곳이었다. 언제나 혼자였던 그녀 앞에 어느 날 배 한 척이 나타났다. 태풍에 휩쓸려 항로를 이탈한 배는 겨우 물에 떠 있었다. 돛대는 부러지고, 돛은 갈기갈기 찢어져 있었다. 미지의 절벽 바위로 표류된 어부들이 할 수 있는 일은 아무것도 없었다. 사실 이곳은 사람을 잡아먹는 외눈박이 거인 '외눈배기'들의 고향이었다. 다행히도 영등이 외눈배기들보다 먼저 어부들을 발견하여 왕바위의 그림자 아래에 숨겨주었다. 얼마 지나지 않아 외눈배기 대장이 나타나 영등에게 맛있는 반찬거리로 가득 찬 어선을 보았느냐고 물었다. 영등은 모르는 척하며, 그런 흔적은 전혀 보지 못했고 그저 바위에 부딪히는 거센 바람에 머리를 말리는 중이라고 둘러댔다.

외눈배기

외눈배기가 떠나자, 어부들은 큰 감사를 표시했다. 며칠 후, 어부들은 배를 고쳐 집으로 돌아갈 준비를 마쳤다. 영등은 배를 더 안전하게 만들어서 떠나는 게 좋겠다고 하였고, 도착해서 닻을 내릴 때까지 '가남보살 가남보살' 염불을 외야한다고 조언했다. 어느덧 그리웠던 고향 땅 제주가 눈앞에 보였다. 어부들은 감격에 겨워 울부짖느라 염불을 외라는 영등의 충고를 잊었고, 다시 회오리바람에 휩쓸려 외눈배기의 땅으로 날아가 버렸다.

다행히 이번에도 영등이 먼저 어부들을 발견했다. 왜 시키는 대로 하지 않았냐며 꾸짖고 다시 한 번 어부들을 숨겨주었다가 바람이 적당해질 때 돌려보냈다. 어부들은 이번에는 염불을 외우는 데 집중했다. 배가 완전히 정박하기 전까지 한라산 봉우리는 쳐다도 보지 않았다. 그러나 정작 영등은 운이 나빠 외눈배기들에게 잡혔다. 반찬거리를 뺏긴 것에 화가 난 외눈배기들은 그 자리에서 영등을 죽이고 시신을 세 부분으로 잘라 바다에 내던졌다. 토막 낸 세 부분의 시신은 제주에 떠내려왔다. 머리는 '우도', 몸통은 '성산', 다리는 '한수리'에 떠올랐다. 영등을 알아본 어부들은 끔찍한 광경에 망연자실하였고, 무당을 불러 영등의 혼을 달래는 큰굿을 벌였다.

그날 밤 파도에서 신비한 안개가 피어났다. 바람이 온 섬을 휘돌았다. 안개가 걷히자 영등의 몸이 다시 꿰매어져 있었다. 영등의 몸이 한 송이 꽃봉오리처럼 떠올랐고, 제주 곳곳에 따스한 생명의 바람이 불었다. 이후부터 영등은 일 년에 한 번씩 부활하여 15일 동안 제주 섬 곳곳을 돌보며 얼어붙은 겨울을 쫓아내고, 봄의 숨결을 불어들이며, 새로운 생명의 씨앗을 바다에 뿌려주었다.[102]

영등신이 북쪽 해안을 보호하고 있는 한편, 남쪽 해안에서는 여러 귀신이 출몰하여 사람들을 괴롭히고 있었다. 그중 거대한 화산 바위 형상을 한 귀신 '홀어멍돌'이 있었다. 용암이 흘러내려 마른 자국이 남아있는 이 바위는 신산리 해안의 대부분을 차지하고 있다. 굳어진 용암 덩어리는 오래전부터 마을 주민들에게 원한이 있었는지, 이 동네 바다에서는 사고가 끊이지 않았다고 한다. 이상하게도 희생자는 항상 남자였다. 사고로 죽은 남자들이 전부 홀어멍돌이 보이는 집에 살았다는 것을 깨달은 사람들은 바위에 의심을 품기 시작했다.

사람들은 바위를 깨뜨려 없애

홀어멍돌

지 않고, 바위의 원망을 풀어주는 것을 선택했다. 사람들은 바위가 남편이 있는 아내들을 질투하여 남자들을 죽인 것으로 생각해 바위의 짝을 만들어주기로 했다. 마을 한가운데에 있는 언덕 꼭대기에 남근을 상징하는 '남근석'을 세웠다. 더 이상 홀어멍이 아닌 바위는 그 뒤로 남자들을 죽이지 않았고, 사람들과 조화롭게 살았다는 전설이 있다.[103] 이러한 마을 사람들의 생각이 이상해 보일 수 있지만 전례가 없는 일은 아니었다. 현재까지도 음기가 과잉된 장소와 물건은 위험하여 양기와 균형을 이루어야 한다고 생각하는 경향이 있다. 이러한 이유로 남근을 형상화한 돌을 음기가 강한 곳에 두게 된 것이다.

제주 남서쪽 해안의 마라도는 음기가 강한 곳이다. 이곳에는 원한을 품은 한 십 대 소녀의 혼령이 살고 있다. 마라도는 관의 형태를 닮았다고 하여 보기만 해도 부정적인 기운을 받는다고 생각했다. 그래서 마라도가 보이는 제주 남서쪽에 사는 사람들은 무덤들 주위로 섬이 보이지 않도록 높은 돌담을 쌓았다.[104] 마라도의 유명한 짜장면집 도보 5분 거리에 '애기업개 할망당'이 있다. 그러나 이곳은 이름과 달리 할머니의 집이 아니라 열네 살 소녀의 영혼을 기리

애기업개

는 사당이다.

    옛날 옛적 소녀 '허씨아기'가 길가에 버려졌다. 소녀는 살아남기 위해 다른 아이들을 업어 돌보는 일을 하면서부터 '애기업개'라고 불리게 되었다. 소녀는 열네 살 때 해녀들을 따라 마라도로 가는 배를 탔다. 마라도에 짐을 풀자마자 파도가 너무 세서 물질을 할 수 없었다. 다시 떠날 준비를 했는데, 폭풍우가 불어 섬에 발이 묶였다. 하루는 해녀의 꿈에 산신대왕이 나타나 열네 살 처녀를 섬에 두고 가면 배를 띄울 수 있다고 말했다. 다음날 다른 해녀들에게 꿈에 대해 이야기했다. 같은 처지의 동료를 남기고 떠나는 일은 너무 잔인하다는 생각이 들었지만, 이대로 있으면 모두 굶어 죽겠다는 생각에 산신대왕의 말대로 애기업개를 두고 배에 올랐다. 애기업개에게는 섬 저편에 두고 온 포대기를 가져오라고 둘러대며 주의를 돌렸다. 해녀들이 떠나자, 풍랑은 잠잠해졌다. 떠난 이들은 살 기회를 얻었으나 애기업개는 황량한 섬에 홀로 남겨졌다. 이듬해 사람들이 마라도를 찾았으나 불쌍한 애기업개는 이미 오래전에 굶어 죽은 뒤였다. 까마귀가 뜯어갔는지 뼈만 남았다. 애기업개의 원통한 영혼을 달래기 위해 매년 제사를 올리며 처녀당을 세웠다. 이것이 오늘날 애기업개할망당이 되었다.[105]

버려지는 아픔을 너무나 잘 알고 있는 또 다른 바다의 신이 있다. 김녕리에 있는 '쌍둥이 미륵돌'이다. 김녕 서문하르방당 봉분에는 쌍둥이 미륵돌이 어떻게 발견되었는지, 그리고 마을 어부 윤씨하르방에게 어떻게 버려졌는지에 대한 사연이 기록되어 있다.

어느 날 낚시를 하러 바다로 나간 윤씨는 물고기를 한 마리도 잡지 못했다. 대신 이상한 모양의 돌을 하나 낚았다. 실망은 곧 경이로 바뀌었다. 돌이 모습을 드러내는 순간 주위로 물거품이 일었고, 기이한 빛이 바위에서 뿜어져 나오는 듯했다. 그날부터 윤씨하르방의 운명은 바뀌었다. 배를 타고 나갈 때마다 몇 번이나 갈치를 통째로 낚는 행운이 찾아왔다. 얼마 지나지 않아 이상한 돌 하나를 또 낚았다. 그는 잠시 생각에 잠겼다. 상서로운 징조로 여기고 배 한 쪽에 돌을 위한 작은 사당을 만들었다. 그때부터 윤씨하르방은 온갖 종류의 희귀하고 값비싼 물고기들을 낚기 시작했다. 그러나 얼마 지나지 않아 이 돌의 가치를 다시 생각하게 되었다. 그의 배는 그렇게 크지 않았고, 만약 자리를 차지하는 돌을 치워버리면 그 자리에 물고기를 더 많이 채워 넣을 수 있겠다는 생각에 짜증이 나기 시작했다. 윤씨하르방은 돌을 다시 바다로 던져버렸다.

그것은 우매한 결정이었다. 바로 다음 날 끔찍한 폭풍우가 마을을 강타했다. 폭풍은 보름 동안 계속되었고, 날이 갈수록 더 강력해졌다. 조업을 나설 수 없게 되었고, 집과 지붕이 날아가고 논밭이 물에 잠겨 기근이 들 위기였다. 다행인 것은 버려진 미륵돌이 아량을 베풀 줄 아는 신이었다는 것이다. 폭풍우가 몰아치던 어느 밤, 윤씨하르방의 꿈속에 백발노인이 나타났다. 노인은 추위 때문에 머리부터 발끝까지 떨면서 불쌍한 모습을 한 채 따뜻한 곳에 집을 마련해줄 수 있냐고 간청했다. 노인은 사실 차가운 바닷속에 버려져 있던 두 개의 미륵돌 중 하나였다. 노인은 바다는 나의 진정한 고향이 아니니 육지 어딘가에 안치해 주면 사람들에게 온갖 복을 내려주겠다고 말했다.

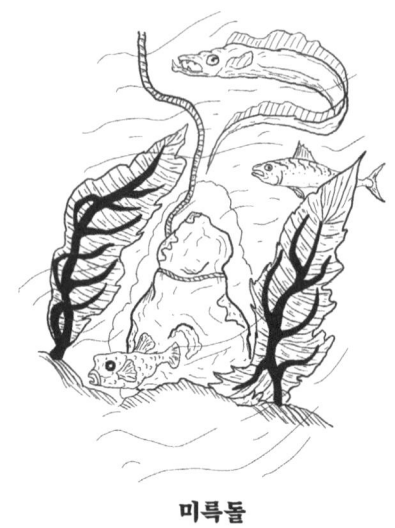

미륵돌

◆ 자식이 없는 사람들에게 '산신(産神)'이 되어주겠다.
　(여기서 산은 자연물 산(山)이 아니라,
　'태어나다'는 의미의 산(産)을 뜻한다.)

◆ 집안의 평화를 원하는 사람들에게
　'수신(守神, 수호신)'이 되어주겠다.

◆ 가난한 사람에게는 '재물신(財物神)'이 되어주겠다.

간청을 마친 백발노인은 바다로 돌아갔다. 다음날 윤씨하르방은 일어나자마자 포구로 달려갔다. 폭풍우와 차가운 바닷물에도 아랑곳하지 않고 미륵돌을 찾으러 깊은 바닷속으로 뛰어들었다. 그런데 드러누워 있으리라 생각했던 미륵돌이 모래 위에 서 있었다. 윤씨하르방은 돌미륵을 건져다 '영등물'이라고 불리는 양지바른 곳에 돌로 제단을 둘러 모셨다. 미륵돌들은 지금도 남아있다. 미륵돌을 숭배하면 부귀와 다산을 가져다주며, 제주와 육지를 안전하게 오갈 수 있게 해준다고 전해진다.[106] 미륵돌은 제주에서 바다 신으로 모셔졌으나, 정작 이름은 바다와 관련이 없는 것이 이상하다. 미륵은 산스크리트어 मैत्रेय(마이트레야)에서 왔다. 엄밀히 말하면 미륵은 신이라기보다 석가모니의 뒤를 이을 미래의 부처에 가깝다고 볼 수 있다.[107]

12장.
도깨비 카드

~~~~~~~~~~~~~~

백마 피와 수수밥
오소리 잡놈
띠배

백마 피와 수수밥

도깨비는 한반도 신화에 등장하는 여러 상상 속 존재 중에서도 가장 독특하고 한국적인 존재다. 대개 몽둥이를 휘둘러 물건을 변신시키거나 뭘 만들어내는 장난기 많고 익살스러운 모습의 도깨비에는 익숙하지만 도깨비를 숭배의 대상으로 삼았다는 사실은 잘 모른다. 육지 사람들에게 도깨비는 민담에 나오는 장난꾸러기 같은 존재겠지만, 제주에서는 부와 풍요, 만선 등 여러 복을 가져다준다고 여겨 숭배했다. 그렇다고 도깨비를 마냥 숭배하는 것도 아니었다. 왜냐하면 그들은 변덕이 엄청나게 심해서 주위 사람에게 악영향을 주기도 했기 때문이다. 그래서 신주를 모시는 사람의 올바른 도구와 마음가짐이 중요했다. 낙천리 도깨비당 본풀이의 주인공 '송영감'이 그런 사람이었다.

만주 출신 농민 송영감은 약초를 캐어 근근이 생계를 이어가고 있었는데, 도깨비가 나타나 부자로 만들어 주겠다는 말에 현혹되었다. 도깨비 삼형제는 제사를 지내달라고 청했고, 송영감은 한달음에 나가서 돼지 한 마리를 잡아 수수밥, 수수떡과 함께 바쳤다. 제사상에 만족한 도깨비들은 흔쾌히 송영감과의 약속을 지켰다. 한때 움막에서 살았을 정도로 마을에서 가장 가난했던 송영감은 어느새 기와집에 사는 부자가 되었다. 그러나 아무리 집이 넓어도 도깨비 셋과 함께 살다 보니 비좁게 느껴졌다. 송영감은 도깨비들한테 받은 은혜는 잊고 원망하는 마음만 커졌다. 만나는 사람마다 도깨비랑 사는 것이 어떠냐 귀찮게 물어보는 데다 이상하게 예전보다 잘 먹는데 오히려 살이 빠지고 하루하루 점점 더 쇠약해졌다. 이게 다 도깨비 때문이라고 생각했다. 송영감은 도깨비를 쫓아낼 계획을 세웠다.

어느날 도깨비들을 모아놓고 내기를 제안했다. 하루만에 넓은 밭의 수확물을 모두 문밖에 두면 평생 도깨비들을 섬길 것이오, 실패한다면 이제 그만 내 집을 떠나라고 했다. 당연히 성공할거라 믿은 도깨비들은 흔쾌히 응했다.

그러나 그것은 도깨비들의 근거 없는 자신감이었다. 해 질 무렵이 되어서도 작업이 끝날 기미가 보이지 않았다. 도깨비 삼형제와 송영감의 위상이 바뀌는 순간이었다. 오랫동안 두려워했던 도깨비들을 드디어 손아귀에 넣게 된 것이다. 송영감은 이 기회에 아예 도깨비들을 없애기로 결심했다. 지칠대로 지친 도깨비 삼형제를 세 그루의 나무에 각각 묶은 후 네 등분으로 토막내 집에서 멀리 떨어진 곳에 흩뿌렸다. 혹시나 도깨비 영혼들이 복수하러 돌아올까봐 백마를 도살하여 집안 곳곳에 백마피를 뿌려 안전한 요새를 만들었다.

중국의 십이지 열두 동물은 각자 오행 중 하나에 해당하는데, 말은 불의 동물, 양기를 발산하는 동물로 알려져 있다.[108] 음기를 가진 귀신, 도깨비 같은 존재를 쫓아내기에 제격이었다. 여기에 흰색은 한국 사람들이 오래전부터 신성하게 여기던 색이었다. '흰 백(白)'은 '날 일(日)'자와 한 획 차이가 난다. '날 일(日)'은 태양을 형상화한 글자로 '날', '해', '낮'을 뜻한다. 따라서 흰색은 밝음과 하늘을 상징하는 색이 되었다. 흰 동물을 상서로운 것으로 생각해서, 옛날 한국 사람들은 하늘에 맹세할 때 백마를 제물로 바쳤다.[109] 백마의 머리에는 양기를 상징하는 불과 하늘이 둘 다 있어서 양기를 배로 갖고 있다고 여겼다.

그렇다면 토막 난 도깨비는 어떻게 되었을까. 너무 안타까워할 필요는 없다. 열두 조각으로 토막 난 도깨비 삼형제는 각각 새로운 도깨비가 되어 열두 도깨비로 불어나 사방으로 흩어져 각자의 자리에 좌정했다. 열두 도깨비 중 막내 삼형제는 방황하다가 제주로 들어와 낙선리의 조상신으로 모셔졌다. 그들은 각각 뱃선왕(배의 왕), 산신일월또(산신 조상), 솥불미(가마솥과 방울의 신)가 되었다.[110]

오소리 잡놈

그렇게 제주로 돌아온 도깨비 중 난잡하기로 악명 높은 '오소리 잡놈'이 있었다. 오소리 잡놈과 그의 여섯 형제는 고향 서울에서 추방당할 정도로 말썽꾸러기였다. 막내 오소리 잡놈은 키가 크고 잘생겼지만, 가장 나쁜 난봉꾼이었다. 온갖 곳을 돌아다녀 조선 팔도에 안 가본 곳이 없는 그에게 남은 행선지는 단 하나, 제주였다. 오소리 잡놈이 제주에서 가장 마음에 들었던 점은 여자가 많다는 것이었다.

어느 날 예쁘고 젊은 해녀 한 명이 눈에 띄었다. 일찍이 과부가 되어 지켜줄 사람이 없던 해녀는 오소리 잡놈의 먹잇감이 되었다. 해녀의 집에 따라간 오소리 잡놈은 밤이 되자 해녀의 침실로 기어들어갔다. 그날 이후 해녀는 점점 쇠약해졌고, 더 이상 물질을 나갈 수도 없게 되었다. 이웃사람이 걱정하여 마을 심방에게 알렸다.

이 소식은 오소리 잡놈의 여섯 형제들의 귀에도 전해졌다. 그들 역시 제주에서 '영감'이라 불리는 도깨비들이었다. 형제들은 오소리 잡놈을 찾아 나섰다. 가시덤불이 우거진 '곶자왈', 바위로 뒤덮인 '빌레왓', 큰 돌무더기 '한머들'을 훑어도 보이지 않았다. 할 수 없이 마을로 내려오는데 어디선가 굿하는 소리가 들려왔다. 누군가 부르는 듯한 소리가 들려 귀를 기울였다. 언덕 너머에서 "영감 영감"하는 소리가 울려 퍼졌다. 굿이 시작되는 소리였다.

영감놀이의 도입부를 '초감제'라고 한다. 영감을 굿판

으로 소환하는 의식으로, 종이탈과 검은색 외투를 입고 갓을 쓴 채 횃불을 휘두르며 영감의 행렬을 흉내낸다. 여섯 도깨비는 자신들을 위한 음식과 술이 차려져 있으니 나타나길 마다할 이유가 없었다. 여섯 영감은 잔치의 대가로 죽음을 눈앞에 둔 해녀를 보며 오소리 잡놈의 무자비한 행동을 꾸짖으며 불쌍한 과부에게서 당장 떨어지라고 말했다. 그러자 오소리 잡놈이 나타나 과부를 괴롭힌 것을 반성했다. 도깨비들은 무당에게 앞으로도 잘 대접해 주면 사람들을 이롭게 할 것이라고 말했다. 그 말에 무당이 잔치를 준비하자 도깨비들은 흥이 나서 춤을 추기 시작했다. 조금 전까지만 해도 죽기 직전이었던 과부도 일어나 춤을 추었다. 동네 사람들도 동참하여 어린 무당 소미의 북소리에 박자를 맞추어 춤을 추니 순식간에 해녀 과부의 집은 흥겨운 잔치판이 되었다. 얼마 지나지 않아 도깨비들의 시선이 밖에 있는 짚배로 향했다. 짚배에는 돼지고기, 수수밥, 수수떡 등 도깨비들이 좋아하는 음식이 가득 담겨 있었다. 무당은 당신들을 위해 준비한 배방선(제물을 가득 담은 짚배)이라고 설명했다. 이것이 영감놀이의 세 번째 단계인 '막푸다시'다. 이때 도깨비 형제

12장. 도깨비 카드

띠배

들은 이름 없는 잡귀들과 함께 배에 오르라는 권유를 받는다.

도깨비들이 승선하면 영감놀이의 마지막 단계 '도진'이 시작된다. 이때 띠배(배방선)는 이곳을 떠나 먼 바다로 가게 되고, 배에 탄 도깨비와 그들이 몰고 온 질병도 같이 떠난다. 이러한 의식은 '영감놀이'로 전승되었다.[111]

공존의 섬, 제주

오소리 잡놈 같은 악한 존재에게도 호화로운 연회를 베풀어 주는 곳이라면, 제주에서 환영받지 못할 이는 없을 것이다. 우리가 살펴본 이야기에는 갈등을 다룬 것도 많지만, 제주 신화를 설명하는 주된 주제는 '공존'이라고 할 수 있다. 소동이 잦아들고 나면 패배한 공격자도 새로운 역할을 맡아, 한때 자신이 쑥대밭으로 만들었던 세상에게 도움을 베풀며 살아갈 수 있게 되었다.

아이들에게 저주를 내리던 구삼승할망은 이제 저승에 있는 영혼들을 돌본다. 한때 자신의 주인을 위협하던 정수남이는 이제 가축의 수호신이 되어 그녀를 돕고 있다. 심지어 외지에서 온 침략자인 김통정은 제주인들이 가장 필요로 하는 것을 그들에게 주었다. 어떤 전설에 따르면, 김통정은 섬을 떠나기 직전까지도 주민들에 대한 걱정으로 가득했다고 한다. 그간 섬에 끼친 피해를 보상하기 위해 그는 해안가 바위 위에 자신의 발을 쾅 소리나게 올렸다. 그러자 바위가 둘로 갈라지면서 샘이 솟아났는데, 고성리 사람들은 지금까지 그 샘물을 마시고 있다고 한다.[112]

제주 사람들의 공존에 대한 굳은 믿음을 가장 잘 보여주는 것은 그들의 신이 기거하는 곳이다. 남선비의 두 아내인 여산부인과 노일제대귀일의 딸이 한 지붕 아래 살 수 있다면, 세상에 봉합되지 않을 갈등은 없을 것이다.

그런데 무속신만 한집에 사는 것은 아니다. 심지어 다른 종교의 신들도 제주에서는 다같이 어울려 산다. 실제로 한 신을 숭배할 때 한반도의 주요 신앙인 샤머니즘, 불교, 유교 요소가 모두 섞이는 경우도 있다. 가장 대표적인 예는 제주 북부 화천동에 있는 다섯 개의 미륵돌을 모신 사당이다. 화천사 뒤에 있는 이 오신상은 언뜻 평범한 바위로 보인다. 하지만 자세히 들여다보면 사람 얼굴 윤곽 형태처럼 자연스럽게 깎아진 것을 발견할 수 있다. 둥근 몸체 덩어리 위로 뾰족한 머리가 있으며 얼굴 부분의 돌출된 부분은 '코'처럼 보인다. 석상들은 마치 자연과 인간의 합작품처럼, 모방할 수 없는 고유한 정체성을 각자 지니고 있다. 이들의 이름이 '미륵'인 것을 보면 불교에 기원을 두고 있는 것으로 보인다. '미륵'은 불교에서 유래한 것으로, 미래의 부처를 의미한다. 사찰 뒤에 있는 돌들을 무속신앙이라고 없애지 않았다. 원래 오신상은 절이 생기기 전부터 있었고 불교의 미륵과는 관련이 없었다. 그들이 형상화한 미륵은 제주의 수호신으로서 임신과 출산을 돕는 마을신인 '당신'이었다. 그런 까닭에 마을제를 이곳에서 지냈다. 그런데 마을제의 형식은 불교적이지도, 샤머니즘적이지도 않았다. 오히려 유교

식 마을제인 '포제(酺祭)' 형식을 갖춰서 우리를 더 헷갈리게 만든다. 그러나 제의의 이름은 불교적 의미가 깃든 '석불제'라고 지었다.[113] 그런 점에서 화천사는 제주와 육지의 전통 신앙 생활이 모두 압축되어 있는 곳이라고 할 수 있겠다. 외래 신앙이 뿌리를 내릴 때도 한국의 정신은 그대로 남아 있었다. 불교는 제주의 토속 신앙을 기꺼이 받아들였고, 조선의 설립 이념인 유교는 처음에는 배척했지만 결국 민중들의 뜻을 들어줄 수밖에 없었다.

나는 어떠냐고? 제주와 한국의 매력에 두손 두발 다 들었다. 이곳의 사람과 신도 나를 그렇게 봐 주길 바랄 뿐이다. 강제로 짚배에 실리고 싶진 않으니까.

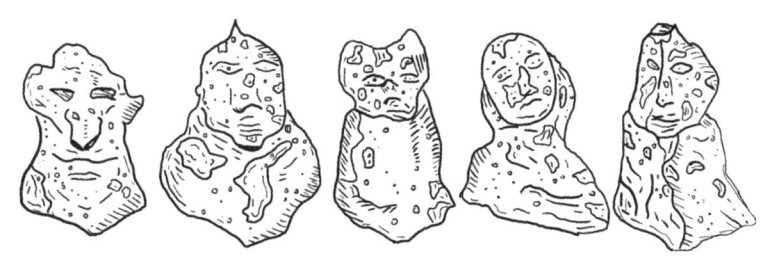

화천사 오신상

주

1 Kim Hogarth, Hyun-key: 'Gut, the Korean Shamanistic Ritual' (Korean Studies Series No. 43, Jimoondang, 2009), p. 309.
2 임준성,「금남최부(錦南崔溥)의 <탐라시삼십오절(耽羅詩三十五絶)> 연구」, 한국시가문화연구(구 한국고시가문화연구), 2011, pp. 301-302.
3 『고려사』 권 57, 지리지, 전라도 탐라현.
4 최열,『옛 그림으로 본 제주』, 혜화 1117, 2021, p. 85.
5 유홍준,『나의 문화유산답사기-제주편』, 창비, 2012, p. 32.
6 한진오,『제주 동쪽- 구좌읍, 남원읍, 성산읍, 우도면, 조천읍, 표선면』, 21세기북스, 2021, p. 24.
7 김유정,『제주 돌담』, 대원사, 2019, pp. 123-124.
8 김유정, 앞의 책, p. 125.
9 송언근,『지리로 가는 제주의 역사, 문화, 생태 답사』, 교육과학사, 2020, p. 128.
10 홍죽희, 여연,『제주 당신을 만나다』, 알렙, 2020, p. 15.
11 김유정,『제주 돌담』, 대원사, 2019, p. 144-145.
12 송언근,『지리로 가는 제주의 역사, 문화, 생태 답사』, 교육과학사, 2020, p. 125, 김유정, 앞의 책, p. 142.
13 Kim, Eugene; Koehler, Robert: 'Joseon's Royal Heritage: 500 Years of Splendor' (Korea Essentials No.7, Seoul Selection, 2011), p. 68.
14 이윤형, 고광민,『제주의 돌문화』, 제주돌문화공원, 2006, p. 221.
15 이윤형, 고광민, 앞의 책, p. 221.
16 무라야마 지쥰,『조선의 귀신』, 문예신서34, 2008, pp. 407-412.
17 김두규,『우리 풍수 이야기』, 북하우스, 2003, 2012(5쇄), p. 85-89.
18 무라야마 지쥰,『조선의 귀신』, 문예신서34, 2008, pp. 412-413.
19 강순희,『제주 신화의 숲』, 한그루, 2022, p. 56.
20 나라키 스에자네,『조선의 미신과 풍속』, 민속원, 2010, 김희영 옮김,

p. 78, p. 97.

21 강순희, 『제주 신화의 숲』, 한그루, 2022, pp. 50-56.

22 최상수, 『세시풍속』, 서문당, 1988, p. 99.

23 정석풍수연구학회, 『풍수 유적 답사기- 감여의 비밀을 찾아서』, 청어람 M&B, 2020, p. 333.

24 최상수, 『세시풍속』, 서문당, 1988, pp. 99-101.

25 임승범, 『해원을 위한 저승길 여정』, 민속원, 2021, p. 63.

26 임승범, 앞의 책, p.18.

27 진성기, 『제주도 무속논고- 남국의 무속』, 민속원, 2002, p. 45.

28 '손각귀신' 혹은 '처녀귀신'이라고도 부른다.

29 Martin, Diana: 'Chinese Ghost Marriage' (1991, Published in JASO 'Occasional Papers' No. 8), Edited by Hugh D.R. Baker and Stephan Feuchtwang, pp. 25-43, University of Oxford, p. 26.

30 이능화, 『조선무속논고- 역사로 본 한국 무속』, 서영대 옮김, 창비, 2008, 2021(6쇄), p. 329.

31 신예경, 문희숙, 『조근조근 제주 신화 2: 자청비부터 도깨비까지, 우리 신화로 배우는 삶과 사랑 이야기』, 지노, 2018, pp. 171-186.

32 현용준, 『제주도 신화』, 서문당, 2016(3쇄), pp. 11-21, 여연, 『조근조근 제주 신화 1: 천지왕부터 설문대할망까지, 우리 신화로 배우는 문화 창조 이야기』, 지노, 2018, pp. 20-37, 김순이, 『제주 신화- 원형을 살려내고 반듯하게 풀어내다』, 여름 언덕, 2020, pp. 65-72, 신동흔, 『살아있는 우리 신화- 우리 신들의 귀환을 위한 이야기 열두 마당』, 한겨레신문사, 2004, pp. 19-34.

33 Dubois, Thomas A: 'An Introduction to Shamanism' (Cambridge University Press, 2009), p. 83.

34 진성기, 『제주도 무속논고- 남국의 무속』, 민속원, 2003, pp. 68-71.

35 여연, 『조근조근 제주 신화 1: 천지왕부터 설문대할망까지, 우리 신화로 배우는 문화 창조 이야기』, 지노, 2018, p. 99.

36 진성기, 『제주도 무속논고- 남국의 무속』, 민속원, 2003, p. 70.

37 Chung Myung-sub (Editor): 'Encyclopaedia of Korean Folk Literature Vol III' (The National Folk Museum of Korea, 2014), p. 82.
38 여연,『조근조근 제주 신화 1: 천지왕부터 설문대할망까지, 우리 신화로 배우는 문화 창조 이야기』, 지노, 2018, p. 4.
39 한진오,『모든 것의 처음, 신화』, 한그루, 2019, pp. 33-34.
40 (한국무속학회) 강소전, 심상교, 양종승, 윤동환, 이명숙, 이승범, 최진아, 하효길,『무구의 이해』, 민속원, 2011, pp. 225-226.
41 한진오,『모든 것의 처음, 신화』, 한그루, 2019, p. 37.
42 여연,『조근조근 제주 신화 1: 천지왕부터 설문대할망까지, 우리 신화로 배우는 문화 창조 이야기』, 지노, 2018, p. 105.
43 Yi Yong Bhum: 'Shamanism' in Yi Yong Bhum, Lee Kyung Yup, Choi Jong Seong, Walraven Boudewjin: 'Korean Popular Beliefs'(Jimoondang, 2015), pp. 105.
44 Cho, Suk-Joon: 'Korean Administration and Organizational Culture' (Kong and Park USA, 2022), pp. 103-104.
45 Walraven, Boudewijn: 'Popular Religion in a Confucianized Society' in Kim Haboush, Jahyun and Deuchler, Martina: 'Culture and the State in Late Choson Korea' (Harvard University Press, 1999), p. 167.
46 Deuchler, Martina: 'The Confucian Transformation of Korea- A Study of Society and Ideology' (Harvard University Press, 1992), p. 175.
47 Walraven, Boudewijn: 'Popular Religion in a Confucianized Society' in Kim Haboush, Jahyun and Deuchler, Martina: 'Culture and the State in Late Choson Korea'(Harvard University Press, 1999), pp. 175-177.
48 한승훈,『무당과 유생의 대결』, 도서출판 사우, 2021, p. 8.
49 하순애,『제주도 신당 이야기』, 한그루, 2024(개정판), p. 129.
50 최열,『옛 그림으로 본 제주』, 혜화 1117, 2021, p. 97.

51 최열, 앞의 책, p. 96

52 현용준, 『제주도 전설』, 서문문고, 1996, 2016(3쇄), pp. 245-246.

53 여연, 『조근조근 제주 신화 1: 천지왕부터 설문대할망까지, 우리 신화로 배우는 문화 창조 이야기』, 지노, 2018, pp. 223-225, 여연, 문무병, 『신화와 함께하는 제주 당올레』, 알렙, 2017, pp. 200-201.

54 진성기, 『제주도 무속논고- 남국의 무속』, 민속원, 2003, p. 189.

55 진성기, 앞의 책, p. 185.

56 여연, 『조근조근 신화 3: 가믄장아기부터 강림차사까지, 우리 신화로 배우는 운명과 도전 이야기』, 지노, 2018, pp. 202-204, (한국무속학회)강소전, 심상교, 양종승, 윤동환, 이명숙, 이승범, 최진아, 하효길, 『무구의 이해』, 민속원, 2011, p. 208.

57 조성제, 『상고사 속의 무속 이야기』, 도서출판 나루터, 2016, pp. 231-233.

58 우종선, 『서낭당, 민속예술연구지 제 5 집』(2020, 한국민속극박물관), p. 51

59 많은 본풀이에서는 인물의 성별이 구체적으로 나오지 않고, 그들의 직함이나 직업으로만 언급된다.

60 여연, 『조근조근 제주 신화 1: 천지왕부터 설문대할망까지, 우리 신화로 배우는 문화 창조 이야기』, 지노, 2018, pp. 223-235, 문무병, 『신화 함께하는 제주당올레』, 알렙, 2017, pp. 200-207.

61 진성기, 『제주도 무속논고- 남국의 무속』, 민속원, 2003, p. 198.

62 현용준, 『제주도 신화』, 서문당, 2016(3쇄), pp. 207-209, 진성기, 『제주도 무속논고- 남국의 무속』, 민속원, 2003, pp. 201-202, 허남춘, 『설문대할망과 제주신화』, 민속원, 2011, p. 223, 김순란, 『이토록 신비로운 제주 신화』, 나무늘보, 2017, pp. 163-169.

63 진성기, 『1960년대를 중심으로 제주무속학 사진집-1- 복을 비는 사람들』, 도서출판 디딤돌, 2008, pp. 67-68.

64 한진오, 『모든 것의 처음, 신화』, 한그루, 2019, p. 293.

65 허남춘, 『설문대할망과 제주신화』, 민속원, 2017, p. 150.

66 신예경, 문희숙, 『조근조근 제주 신화 2: 자청비부터 도깨비까지, 우리 신화로 배우는 삶과 사랑 이야기』, 지노, 2018, pp. 228-229.

67 신예경, 문희숙, 앞의 책, pp. 191-213,
    김순란,『이토록 신비로운 제주신화』, 나무늘보, 2017, pp. 151-160,
    한진오,『모든 것의 처음, 신화』, 한그루, 2019, p. 292, 현용준,
    『제주도 신화』, 서문당, 2016(3쇄), pp. 182-198.
68 나라키 스에자네,『조선의 미신과 풍속』, 민속원, 2010, 김희영 옮김, p. 59.
69 고제희,『대한민국 1% 부자의 길로 가는 시크릿 풍수』, 북이십일, 2020,
    p. 193.
70 어쩌면 여전히 살아있을 수도?
71 김순란,『이토록 신비로운 제주 신화』, 나무늘보, 2017, pp. 117-121,
    현용준,『제주도 신화』, 서문당, 2016 (3쇄), pp. 133-141, 문희숙,
    신예경,『조근조근 제주 신화 2: 자청비부터 도깨비까지,
    우리 신화로 배우는 삶과 사랑 이야기』, 지노, 2018, pp. 153-165.
72 현용준, 앞의 책, pp. 87-133, 여연,『조근조근 제주신화 3:
    가믄장아기부터 강림차사까지, 우리 신화로 배우는 운명과 도전 이야기』,
    지노, 2018, pp. 57-134, 신동흔,『살아있는 우리 신화- 우리 신들의
    귀환을 위한 이야기 열두 마당』, 한겨레신문사, 2004, pp. 140-161.
73 Kim Seong-Nae: 'Shamanic Epics and Narrative Construction of
    Identity on Cheju Island' (Asian Folklore Studies, Vol. 63, No. 1 (2004),
    p. 60.
74 유홍준,『나의 문화유산답사기- 제주편』, 창비, 2012, p. 37.
75 여연, 문무병,『신화와 함께하는 제주 당올레』, 알렙, 2017, pp. 17-27.
    홍죽희, 여연,『제주 당신을 만나다』, 알렙, 2020, pp. 166-169. 여연,
    『조근조근 제주 신화 1: 천지왕부터 설문대할망까지, 우리 신화로 배우는
    문화 창조 이야기』, 지노, 2018, pp. 187-206. 현용준,『제주도 전설』,
    서문문고, 1996, 2016(3쇄), pp. 246-248. 김순이,『제주 신화- 원형을
    살려내고 반듯하게 풀어내다』, 여름 언덕, 2020, pp. 327-338.
76 David J. Nemeth(권상철 옮김): 'Rediscovering Hallasan- Jeju Island's
    Traditional Landscape of Sincerity, Mysticism and Adventure(신비, 성실,
    모험의 제주 전통 경관)' (푸른길, purungil, 2019), p. 52.

77　홍죽희, 여연, 『제주 당신을 만나다』, 알렙, 2020, pp. 137-140.
78　인성리 방사탑 2호(제주특별자치도 민속문화재 제B-17호) 안내판.
79　용수마을 방사탑 2호(제주특별자치도 민속문화재 제8-9호) 안내판.
80　고제희, 『대한민국 1% 부자의 길로 가는 시크릿 풍수』, 북이십일, 2020, p. 127.
81　김영돈, 『제주 성읍 마을』, 대원사, 2012, p. 78.
82　이종철, 『한국 민속신앙의 탐구』, 민속원, 2009, pp. 173-178.
83　김영돈, 앞의 책, p. 75.
84　김동관, 『장승 탐구- 장승과 돌하르방의 기원에 대한 탐구』, 아루나, 2023, p. 281.
85　Lee, Peter, Ch'oe, Yeongcho and De Bary, Theodore (Editors): 'Sources of Korean Tradition, Volume 1: From Early Times through the Sixteenth Century' (Columbia University Press, 1997), p. 203.
86　애월면 광령리 고인훈씨로부터 수집한 이야기, 현용준, 『제주도 전설』, 서문당, 1996, 2016(3쇄), p. 101.
87　홍죽희, 여연, 『제주 당신을 만나다』, 알렙, 2020, pp. 185-189.
88　홍죽희, 여연, 앞의 책, pp. 186-187.
89　현용준, 『제주도 전설』, 서문당, 1996, 2016(3쇄), pp. 39-42.
90　우종선, 『서낭당, 민속예술연구지 제 5 집』, 한국민속극박물관, 2020, p. 81.
91　한진오, 『제주 동쪽- 구좌읍, 남원읍, 성산읍, 우도면, 조천읍, 표선면』, 21세기북스, 2021, p. 70.
92　한진오, 『모든 것의 처음, 신화』, 한그루, 2019, p. 154.
93　한진오, 앞의 책, p. 98. Chung Myung-sub (Editor): 'Encyclopaedia of Korean Folk Literature Vol III' (The National Folk Museum of Korea, 2014), p. 309.
94　김순이, 『제주 신화- 원형을 살려내고 반듯하게 풀어내다』, 여름 언덕, 2020, pp. 299-315.
95　허남춘, 『설문대할망과 제주신화』, 민속원, 2017, p. 234.

96 김수란,『이토록 신비로운 제주 신화』, 나무늘보, 2017, pp. 39-47. 김순이,『제주 신화- 원형을 살려내고 반듯하게 풀어내다』, 여름 언덕, 2020, pp. 73-86. 현용준,『제주도 신화』, 서문당, 2016(3쇄), pp. 32-35. 조현설,『우리 신화의 수수께끼』, 한겨레 출판, 2005, pp. 62-66. 신동흔,『살아있는 우리 신화- 우리 신들의 귀환을 위한 이야기 열두 마당』, 한겨레신문사, 2004, p. 66-79.

97 문희숙, 신예경,『조근조근 제주 신화 2: 자청비부터 도깨비까지, 우리 신화로 배우는 삶과 사랑 이야기』, 지노, 2018, pp. 38-39, p. 47.

98 허남춘,『설문대할망과 제주신화』, 민속원, 2011, p. 193.

99 다섯 가지 곡물이 무엇인지는 상당히 다양하나 일반적인 개념의 오곡은 쌀, 콩, 조, 기장, 보리이다. 김호숙, 마석한,『고조선과 동이- 사기, 한서, 삼국지, 후한서로 읽어 보는』, 한국학술정보, 2022, p. 35.에서 인용. 보다 일반적으로 '오곡'이라는 용어는 모든 곡물이나 주요 작물을 통칭할 때도 쓰인다.

100 신예숙, 문희숙,『조근조근 제주 신화 2: 자청비부터 도깨비까지, 우리 신화로 배우는 삶과 사랑 이야기』, 지노, 2018, pp. 51-135. 신동흔,『살아있는 우리 신화- 우리 신들의 귀환을 위한 이야기 열두 마당』, 한겨레신문사, 2004, pp 222-250. 김순이,『제주 신화- 원형을 살려내고 반듯하게 풀어내다』, 여름 언덕, 2020, pp. 201-244. 김익두,『한국신화를 찾아 떠나는 여행- 우리 문화의 근원, 그 오래된 미래의 탐구』, 지식산업사, 2021, pp. 282-304.

101 여연,『조근조근 신화 3: 가믄장아기부터 강림차사까지, 우리 신화로 배우는 운명과 도전 이야기』, 지노, 2018, pp. 162-163

102 김순이,『제주 신화- 원형을 살려내고 반듯하게 풀어내다』, 여름 언덕, 2020, pp. 317-325. 한진오,『모든 것의 처음, 신화』, 한그루, 2019, p. 185. 국립제주박물관,『태풍 고백- 하나의 눈동자를 가진 외눈박이 바람의 고백』, 국립제주박물관, 2020, p. 110.

103 한진오,『모든 것의 처음, 신화』, 한그루, 2019, p. 117-119.

104 김유정,『제주 돌담』, 대원사, 2019, p. 86.

105 여연,『조근조근 신화 3: 가믄장아기보터 강림차사까지, 우리 신화로 배우는 운명과 도전 이야기』, 지노, 2018, p. 172. 고광민,『마라도의 역사와 민속』,한그루, 2007, p.165.
106 김녕 서문하르방당 본풀이를 기록한 종이가 사당에 있는 항아리에 남겨져 있었다. 이 본풀이는 파평윤씨제주도문중회장 교육학박사 윤두호에 의해 제공되었다. 홍죽희, 여연,『제주 당신을 만나다』, 알렙, 2020, pp. 29-32.
107 김삼룡,『미륵불』, 대원사, 2011, pp. 13-15.
108 김광언,『풍수지리(집과마을)』, 대원사, 1993, pp. 43.
109 김선현,『컬러가 내 몸을 바꾼다』, 넥서스 Books, 2009, pp. 67-68.
110 신예경, 문희숙,『조근조근 제주 신화 2: 자청비부터 도깨비까지, 우리 신화로 배우는 삶과 사랑 이야기』, 지노, 2018, pp. 233-236. 여연, 문무병,『신화 함께하는 제주 당올레』, 알렙, 2017, pp. 174-176.
111 김종대,『한국 민간신앙의 전승과 그 의미』, 민속원, 2021, pp. 229-233. 신예경, 문희숙,『조근조근 제주 신화 2: 자청비부터 도깨비까지, 우리 신화로 배우는 삶과 사랑 이야기』, 지노, 2018, pp 237-245.
112 현용준,『제주도 전설』, 서문문고, 1996, 2016(3쇄), pp. 95-99.
113 이영권,『제주 역사 기행』, 한겨레신문사, 2004, pp. 186-187.

색인

이 책은 작가 톰 보렐리가 고안한 동명의 카드 게임을 바탕으로 한다.
게임에 등장하는 52가지 제주 신화 카드를 책과 함께 즐겨 보자.

초록색 가옥 카드
산담 20-22
고팡 53-55, 73
정주목과 정낭 60-62
정지 64
상방 65
흉가 67

노란색 가신 카드
안칠성 52-55
주목지신 58-61
조왕할망 64, 75
문전신 65-66, 75

빨간색 수호신 카드
방울품 50-52
칠성신상과 허멩이 인형 48-50
영집 37-38
신소미 108-109
사만이 조상의 해골 72-74
강림 74-78
영등할망 120-123
띠배 137
방사탑 86-89
돌하르방 87-89, 92
산호 해녀 97-98
삼승할망 104-108
광양당신 94-96
자청비 112-116
미륵돌 126-129, 143
백마 피와 수수밥 132-135

검은색 해로운 신 카드

조상원귀 27
한양일월 27-29
수명장자의 집 29-33
서수왕 따님아기 116-117
애기업개 124-126
천구아구대멩이 45
과양생이 부부 74-77
외눈배기 121-122
홀어멍돌 123
노일제대귀일의 딸 58-65, 142
고내봉의 산신백관 84-85
구삼승할망 106-108, 142
오소리 잡놈 135-137, 142
정수남이 부엉이 113-117, 142
소천국 82-84, 94
김통정 92-95, 142
장길손 99-101, 104

파란색 특수능력카드

침입하는 뿌리 23
뼈에 들끓는 벌레 23-24
이장 23
벌초 24-25
심방 36-39, 43, 49, 52, 136
삼멩두 38-39
이형상 목사 42-44
양씨 목사 44-45, 50

글/그림. 톰 보렐리

영국 킹스 칼리지 런던에서 역사를 공부한 후, 한국에 와서 8년 넘게 살고 있다. 7년간 영어와 역사를 가르치고, 1년 동안 서울대학교에서 한국어를 공부하면서 한국의 역사와 전통에 매료되었다. 지난 4년간 제주도에 살면서 150여 곳이 넘는 신당을 방문했다. 제주의 모든 신당과 신들을 찾아 기록하는 것을 목표로 하고 있다.

이메일. tombowewe@live.co.uk

감수. 조경철

역사학자. 2003년부터 연세대에서 한국사를 가르치며, 나라이름역사연구소를 운영하고 있다. 《나만의 한국사》, 《백제 불교사연구》 《유물시선-돌》등을 썼다. 늘 새로운 시각에서 역사를 바라보고자 한다.

이메일. 12061289yu@gmail.com

번역 감수. 황자운

이화여자대학교 통역번역대학원 번역 전공. 가치 있는 작품이 언어의 날개를 달고 더 넓은 세상과 만나기를 바라며, 방송예술 번역을 주로 하고 있다.

이메일. fromjaun@gmail.com

편집 총괄 및 국문 정리. 조부용

영화 기자로 4년간 일했으며, 현재는 한국 유물을 탐구하여 콘텐츠로 기획하고, 출판과 웹의 형태로 소개하고 있다. 《백제금동대향로 동물백과》, 《유물시선-돌》을 출판했으며, 한국사 뉴스레터 '나만의 한국사 편지'를 운영하고 있다.

탐라의 귀신: 제주의 영원한 수호자들
Ghosts and Gods of Tamna : The Eternal Guardians of Jeju

초판 1쇄 발행 2024년 11월 15일

글/그림 Tom Borrelli (톰 보렐리)
편집 총괄 및 국문 정리 조부용
편집 조부용, 조부나
감수 조경철
번역 감수 황자운
디자인 남선미, 남연주

인쇄 및 제책 엠그래픽스

펴낸곳 유물시선
등록 2023년 1월 23일 제 2023-000003호

이메일 yumooleyes@gmail.com
Instagram @yumool_eyes
X @my_k_history

ISBN 979-11-980204-2-0 (03910)

© 2024, Tom Borrelli

*이 책의 전체 또는 일부를 재사용하려면 저작권자와
유물시선의 동의를 받아야 합니다.
*잘못 만들어진 책은 구입하신 서점에서 바꾸어 드립니다.

※ Note on the Title of the Book

The Korean title of this book, when transliterated into English, is 'The Gwishin of Tamna /탐라의 귀신'. Tamna/탐라 is the original name for the island of Jeju. Gwishin/귀신/鬼神, however, is more ambiguous. Though it is understood by most Koreans today to merely mean 'ghost', it also has a broader meaning. This can be seen in the two Hanja/한자(Chinese characters used in the formation of Korean words) which constitute the word: 鬼 and 神, meaning 'Ghost' and 'God' respectively. Thus, Gwishin can refer to both kinds of beings. But in the title of this book, Gwishin is used in the sense of Cheonjigwishin/천지귀신/天地鬼神 literally meaning 'The Ghosts and Gods of Heaven and Earth'. This refers to all the spiritual beings which exist between heaven and earth. This term has been used in classical texts such as *Samguk Sagi*/삼국사기 the chronicles of the three kingdoms, *Samguk Yusa*/삼국유사 the memorabilia of the three kingdoms, *Goryeosa*/고려사 history of Gorye and *Joseon Wangjo Sillok*/조선왕조실록 the annals of the Joseon dynasty to encompass all supernatural entities.

Ghosts and Gods of Tamna :
The Eternal Guardians of Jeju

Tom Borrelli

In memory of my dear departed grandmother,
Rena Utterson (1925-2024)

Foreword

Up until the age of twenty, I doubt if I had ever spared a thought for Korea. I certainly had no inkling that I would one day be living in Korea and writing a book about its traditional religious beliefs. From as early as I can remember, I had been interested in the mythologies of various countries and cultures, but I had no idea that such a thing as 'Korean Mythology' even existed. When I finally started to learn about Korea in university, it was its modern history which I became acquainted with. Even when I came to live in Korea in the summer of 2016, I had no knowledge of the country's premodern history or traditional culture.

This quickly started to change towards the end of that year. Though I was staying in the small city of Iksan/익산, I was fortunate enough to live next to the city's high-speed KTX train station. Korea's railway network is so well developed that this meant that the entire western side of the country was easily accessible. Almost every weekend I was off on an adventure, touring Buddhist temples nestled in mountain valleys and royal tombs in secluded pine forest glades.

While a resident of Iksan, I was most immersed in the history of Baekje/백제, the kingdom that controlled that area of Korea during the 'Three Kingdoms Period/삼국시대'. Later, when I moved to Ulsan/울산 on the opposite coast, I started to explore the historic sites of Silla/신라, another of the 'Three Kingdoms'.

However, to truly begin to understand Korea's history and traditions, it wasn't a geographical boundary I had to cross; it was a linguistic one. There are some informative books about these topics written in English, but they only scratch the surface. They are also often more focussed on foreign belief systems adopted by Koreans, like Buddhism and Confucianism, rather than the native beliefs of Koreans. It is the latter which I became more interested in, and so it was essential that I knew enough Korean to read and understand books on this topic. For me, this was no easy feat. Only after a year of studying Korean at the Seoul University Language Education Institute, was I finally ready to read all the kinds of books I wanted to read about Korea.

Ironically, the first two books I read in Korean about Korean traditional religious beliefs were both translations: '*The Ghosts and Gods of Joseon*' authored by the Japanese folklorist Murayama Jijun/村山智順 and '*Considerations of Shamanism in Joseon*(조선무속고)' originally written in Hanja(Chinese characters used in the writing of Korean) by the Korean historian and folklorist, Lee Neunghwa(이능화).

Both of those books were written at times when native Korean religious traditions were still thriving or at least better preserved than they are today. To me, they were two halves of a key, a key which unlocked the door to a vibrant, hitherto inaccessible world. They described a Korea as densely populated with spirits as it is with people: teeming with gods of the mountains, gods of the seas, gods of the village, gods in each room of the house, ghosts of people but also ghosts of animals, plants and even everyday objects.

As I read further, I realised that this hidden world, this pantheon of spirits as diverse as that of Ancient Greece and Rome, is still alive and well. Though the traditional home and village and the gods that lived within have certainly diminished, the nexus of Korea's native religion remains: the shamans.

Shamans can be found all across the peninsula, but the historic shrines in which they once worshipped have rapidly disappeared. Village shrines, in particular, fell victim to the New Vilage Movement/새마을운동 of the 1970s. Though primarily a policy to modernise the rural economy, it also involved the repression and destruction of Korean traditional religious practices. What have now been recognised as intangible parts of Korean heritage were then viewed as superstitions harmful to the country's modernisation. *Shinmok*/신목^{divine trees} were cut down, and shamanist idols were destroyed[1].

Only the most remote province of South Korea was spared the worst of the damage: the island of Jeju. Here, village shrines are as ubiquitous as village churches in rural England. However, I knew nothing of this when I was offered a job in Jeju. All I knew about the island was what everyone else knows about it, that it is a volcanic island filled with white sand beaches and tangerine orchards.

That was enough to make me accept the job and move to Jeju, but it wouldn't be what made me stay. More enchanting than its beaches and orchards are its sacred groves. Nowadays, I enjoy nothing more than wandering the island and touring its shrines, putting faces to the names of the gods I have read about.

But during these trips, I have noticed that even here, the old gods are at risk. Certain shrines have been abandoned and promptly swallowed by a tide of undergrowth, and others have been consumed by construction sites. I hope then that this book, albeit in a small way, can spread awareness of the shrines and the intangible heritage they represent.

From the moment I arrived in this country, its people have shown me nothing but kindness and support. This book and the accompanying card game are a testament to this. Neither would have been possible without help from fellow writers Geuljima(글지마) and Yeoneok(연옥), and of course everyone at Yumool-siseon(유물시선) for giving me a chance and assuring that my work saw the light of day.

From the other side of the world, I have also been lucky enough to receive unrelenting encouragement from my family: my brother James, sister Emily, mother Heather and my father Paul, who helped make the first iteration of my card game.

Note on Romanisation

The more I have studied the Korean language, the more I have lost faith in romanisation. Though the Korean script of *Hangeul*/한글 is intuitive compared to other writing systems, the pronunciation of Korean characters is not as simple as many textbooks would have you believe. Furthermore, different books use different forms of romanisation. Worse still, they do not provide the original Korean characters, making it hard for the reader to track down the original word and pronunciation. In this book, I have generally followed the Revised Romanisation system. However, even in this system, there are some ambiguities, so I have made some alterations of my own. I accept, though, that I am not the greatest authority on the Korean language, and so I have always included the original Korean characters so that the readers themselves can interpret the proper pronunciation of the word. Lastly, for the sake of convenience, I have followed certain romanisation conventions which, though I disagree with, have become too entrenched to change: for example, the Korean surname '이'(pronounced as 'ee') written as 'Lee'.

Consonants

Korean	New Korean Revised Romanisation	Notes
ㄱ	g, k	
ㄲ	kk	I would add that this character often sounds more like a double 'g'(gg) sound when it begins a syllable block.
ㄴ	n	
ㄷ	d, t	
ㄸ	tt	In the same way that the 'ㄷ' character is somewhere between a 'd' and a 't' sound, I would say that 'ㄸ' is somewhere between a double 't'(tt) and a double 'd'(dd) sound.
ㄹ	r, l	It always sounds like an 'l' as a bottom consonant (i.e. the consonant at the end of a syllable block in Korean). For example '살'(flesh) would be pronounced 'Sal'. When it follows a syllable block ending in a consonant it can also be pronounced like an 'n'. For example, '왕릉' would be pronounced 'Wang-neung'.
ㅁ	m	
ㅂ	b, p	I would say that this is always closer to sounding like a 'p' at the end of a word. For example '탑'(tower, pagoda) would be pronounced 'Tap'.

ㅃ	pp	I would add that this can also sound like a double 'b' sound(bb).
ㅅ	s	This sounds like an 's' when followed by the ㅏ(a), ㅓ(eo), ㅜ(u/oo), ㅗ(o), ㅡ(eu) vowels but like an 'sh' consonant blend when followed by the ㅣ(i/ee) vowel. If it is the final consonant, it sounds like a 't'.
ㅆ	ss	The same rules apply as above though when it comes before a vowel it is pronounced like a double s sound as in the powerful 's' sound at the start of the word 'son'. If it is the bottom consonant, it sounds like a 't' unless the next syllable block begins with a vowel. For example the infinitive of the verb '있다'(to exist) is pronounced 'itda' as the 'ㅆ' is followed by a consonant 'ㄷ'(d) but the conjugated form '있어'(it/they exist(s)) is pronouncēd Iss-eo as the 'ㅆ' is followed by the vowel 어(eo).
ㅇ	ng	This is silent if it precedes a vowel. If it follows a vowel, it is pronounced like the '-ng' consonant blend. For example the word '강'(river) is pronounced 'Gang'.
ㅈ	j	If it comes at the start of the word, it is pronounced as 'j'. It is also pronounced as a 'j' if it comes at the end of a syllable block and the next syllable block begins with a vowel. If it comes at the end of a word or the end of a syllable block and the next

		block begins with a consonant, it is pronounced as 't'.
ㅉ	jj	The same rules as above but it has a stronger j sound if it comes at the start of a word.
ㅊ	ch	It is pronounced as 'ch' if it begins a word and 't' if it comes at the end of a syllable block.
ㅋ	k	
ㅌ	t	
ㅍ	p	
ㅎ	h	

Vowels

Korean	New Korean Revised Romanisation	Notes
ㅏ	a	
ㅐ	ae	Long 'a' sound as in 'rate'.
ㅑ	ya	
ㅒ	yae	
ㅓ	eo	Short 'u' sound as in 'bun'.
ㅔ	e	Short 'e' sound as in 'get'.
ㅕ	yeo	
ㅖ	ye	
ㅗ	o	
ㅘ	wa	
ㅙ	wae	Same pronunciation as 'way' or 'weigh'.
ㅚ	oe	I would also replace 'oe' with 'we' as the '외' sounds like the 'we' in 'wet'.
ㅛ	yo	
ㅜ	u	In the Revised Romanisation system, this character is expressed as 'u' but I have also written it as 'oo' to distinguish this as a long 'u' sound/double 'o' sound rather than a short 'u' sound.

ㅝ	wo	
ㅞ	we	This is not the 'wee' sound in the word 'we' but rather the 'we' in 'wet'.
ㅟ	wi	This sounds like a long 'e' sound if not followed by a consonant so in this case I have replaced 'wi' with 'wee'.
ㅠ	yu	Long 'u' sound as in 'yule'.
ㅡ	eu	This sounds like the noise one might make if disgusted.
ㅢ	ui	As a combination of two Korean vowels- 'ㅡ' and 'ㅣ' it sounds like 'eu' and 'ee' said in quick succession if it is found at the beginning of a word. If '의' is instead found in the middle of the word it sounds more like a long 'e' sound.
ㅣ	i	This sounds like a short 'i' sound if followed by a consonant but a long 'e' sound if not. Thus, I have sometimes transliterated this as 'ee' instead of 'i'.

로마자/한국어 표기 일러두기

한국어를 공부하면 할수록 로마자 표기에 대한 신뢰가 사라졌다. '한글'은 다른 문자체계에 비해 직관적으로 이해하기 쉽지만, 한국어 발음은 교과서에서 설명하는 것만큼 간단하지 않다. 게다가 책마다 로마자를 다른 형태로 표기하고 있다. 더욱이 한글 원문을 제공하지 않아서 독자가 원어와 발음을 추적하기 어렵다. 이 책은 대체로 개정 로마자 표기법을 따랐다. 그러나 이 체계에서도 모호한 부분이 있어 나름대로 약간 수정한 부분도 있다. 그러나 어쩔수없이 혼동을 줄 수 있는 부분이 있기 때문에 임의로 변경하기에는 이미 고착화된 경우 공식 로마자 표기법을 따랐다. 예를 들어 한국의 성 '이'를 'ee'가 아닌 'Lee'로 표기했다.

자음

한국어	개정 로마자 표기법	참고사항
ㄱ	g, k	
ㄲ	kk	단어 첫머리에 올 때, 종종 'gg'(ㄲ) 소리에 더 가깝게 들린다.
ㄴ	n	
ㄷ	d, t	
ㄸ	tt	'ㄷ'이 'd'와 't' 사이의 발음이듯, 'ㄸ'은 'tt'와 'dd' 사이의 발음에 가깝다.
ㄹ	r, l	받침 자음으로 쓰일 때 'l'처럼 들린다. 예를 들어 'sal/살'은 'sal'로 발음된다. 그러나 'n'처럼 발음될 때도 있다. 예를 들어 '왕릉'은 'Wang-neung/왕능'으로 발음된다.
ㅁ	m	
ㅂ	b, p	'ㅂ' 발음은 단어 끝에 'p'가 붙은 것 같은 소리가 난다. 예를 들어 '탑'은 'tap'과 가깝다.
ㅃ	pp	'ㅃ' 발음은 'bb'와 비슷한 소리로도 발음된다.
ㅅ	s	'ㅅ' 발음은 모음 'ㅏ'(a), 'ㅓ'(eo), 'ㅜ'(u/oo), 'ㅗ'(o), 'ㅡ'(eu)와 만날 때 'sh'처럼

19

		발음되나 받침으로 쓰일 경우에는 't' 처럼 들린다.
ㅆ	ss	모음 앞에 올 때는 위와 같은 규칙이 적용되나 'son'처럼 's' 소리가 강하게 이중 'ss' 소리처럼 들린다. 'ㅆ'이 받침으로 쓰일 때, 다음 음절이 모음으로 시작하지 않는 경우 't'처럼 발음된다. 예를들어 '있다(to exist)'의 경우 'ㅆ' 받침 뒤에 자음 'ㄷ'(d)이 오므로 'itda'로 발음되며, '있어(it/they exist(s))'의 경우 'iss-eo'로 발음된다.
ㅇ	ng	모음 앞에 결합하면 무성음이다. 모음 뒤에 오면 '-ng'으로 발음된다. 예를들어 '강(river)'은 'Gang'으로 발음된다.
ㅈ	j	단어 첫머리에 오면, 'j'로 발음한다. 또한 'ㅈ' 받침 다음 음절이 모음으로 시작할 때도 'j'로 발음된다. 그러나 'ㅈ' 받침 다음 음절이 자음으로 시작할 때는 't'로 발음된다.
ㅉ	jj	'ㅈ'과 같은 규칙을 따르되 단어의 시작 부분에 'ㅉ'이 오면 'j' 음이 강하게 난다.
ㅊ	ch	단어 시작 부분에 쓰일 때는 'ch'로 발음하고, 받침으로 쓰일 때는 't'로 발음한다.
ㅋ	k	
ㅌ	t	
ㅍ	p	
ㅎ	h	

모음

한국어	개정 로마자 표기법	참고사항
ㅏ	a	
ㅐ	ae	'rate' 발음에서와 같이 긴 'a' 소리.
ㅑ	ya	
ㅒ	yae	
ㅓ	eo	'bun' 발음에서와 같이 짧은 'u' 소리.
ㅔ	e	'get' 발음에서와 같이 짧은 'e' 소리.
ㅕ	yeo	
ㅖ	ye	
ㅗ	o	
ㅘ	wa	
ㅙ	wae	'way' 또는 'weigh'와 같은 발음이다.
ㅚ	oe	'ㅚ'를 'oe'로 표기하나 나는 'wet'의 'we'발음처럼 들리기 때문에 'oe'를 'we'로 대체했다.
ㅛ	yo	
ㅜ	u	개정 로마자 표기법에서 이 글자는 'u'로 표현되지만, 짧은 'u' 소리가 아닌

		긴 'u' 소리를 구별하기 위해 'oo'로도 표기했다.
ㅝ	wo	
ㅞ	we	이것은 'we'라는 단어의 'wee' 소리가 아니라 'wet'의 'we' 부분에 해당한다.
ㅟ	wi	받침이 없을 때 소리가 길게 들리는데 이 때에는 'wi'를 'wee'로 대체하였다.
ㅠ	yu	'yule'처럼 긴 'u'로 소리낸다.
ㅡ	eu	이 소리는 마치 역겨울 때 내는 소리처럼 들린다.
ㅢ	ui	'ㅡ'와 'ㅣ' 두 모음의 조합으로, 'eu'와 'ee'를 연속적으로 빠르게 발음하는 소리와 비슷하다. 만약 'ㅢ'가 단어 중간에 있으면 좀 더 긴 'e' 소리가 된다.
ㅣ	i	'ㅣ'가 자음뒤에 올 때 짧게 'i' 소리가 나는데 그렇지 않고 긴 소리로 발음될 경우가 가끔있는데 그럴 때 'i' 대신 'ee'로 음역했다.

Contents

**Chapter One.
Tomb & Ghost Cards**
30

**Chapter Two.
Shaman Cards**
48

**Chapter Three.
Confucian Magistrate Cards**
56

**Chapter Four.
Snake God Cards**
64

**Chapter Five.
Household God Cards**
76

**Chapter Six.
Death God Cards**
92

**Chapter Seven.
Village God Cards**
102

**Chapter Eight.
Jeju Protecting &
Attacking God Cards**
114

**Chapter Nine.
Fertility God Cards**
128

**Chapter Ten.
Farming God Cards**
138

**Chapter Eleven.
Sea God Cards**
148

**Chapter Twelve.
Dokkaebi Cards**
162

**Jeju:
The Island of Coexistence**
174

Index
188

Jeju: The Island of Abundance

Who dug the sacred pond at the top of the cliff?
Clams may open and close their mouths, but only birds may fly.
The towering peak was chiselled away,
forming the crag of Sanbangsan/산방산.
This we know to be true.
And yet there are not many who ask
about this strange landscape.

Dark pines, verdant bamboo, and rosewood incense.
Red chestnuts, yellow Yuja/유자, Yugam/유감 and tangerines.
Even when the white snow is more than a foot deep,
camelias still bloom.
The green glow of spring lasts for all four seasons.

— Excerpt from Tamna Si Samship O Jeol ^{thirty-five poems on Tamna}
by Geumnam Choe Bu[2]

Though small and secluded, Jeju is not to be overlooked. Possessing a unique charm of its own, Jeju is like nowhere else in the world. Yet its official titles give us no clue as to what truly distinguishes the island. From 1294[3], it has been known as *Jeju*/제주, deriving from the Hanja characters '濟州' meaning 'Large county over the water'. Before that, it was most commonly known as *Tamna*/탐라, which is thought to mean simply 'Island Country'.[4]

These, however, are not the only names for the island. There are several far more descriptive unofficial titles that reveal its distinct characteristics. The most famous name among them is *Samdaseom*/삼다섬, 'The Island of Three Abundances', which are known to be rocks, wind and women.

But to me, the true appeal of the island is more immaterial. Though small in size, Jeju looms large on the spiritual plane. It is a treasure trove of not only its own religious beliefs but also those of the mainland. This fourth abundance is captured by yet another of its names: *Mudangdo*/무당도 the island of shamans. This is a fitting name even now with Jeju laying claim to around 250 shrines, 400 shamans, 500 shamanist songs[5], and 18,000 gods.[6]

This does not mean though, that the island is covered in a jumble of grand temples and cathedrals.

The sanctuaries of the gods are generally small and open to the elements; their sacred boundaries are but simple dry-stone walls and their roofs are often just the canopy of the robust Poknang/폭낭^{the hackberry tree}. Such simplicity, however, confirms rather than denies their divinity. Their shrines are not separated from the beauty of the surrounding landscape; they are a part of it.

To those with their eyes opened, the whole island is imbued with divine energy. Its coasts are patrolled by *Yongwang*/용왕^{dragon kings} and caressed by the breath of the *Yeongdeung Halmang*/영등할망^{one of its many wind gods}. Its undulating volcanic hills, the *Oreum*/오름 are topped by shrines to *Sanshin*/산신^{mountain gods}, and the volcano at its centre is the final resting place of the island's creator goddess, the *Seolmundae Halmang*/설문대 할망.

Alas, the presence of so many gods is not merely a result of the natives' appreciation for their environment. It is also a mark of desperation. The islanders have depended so much on the gods because they could depend on nothing else. Though Jeju is abundant in some things, it is severely lacking in others. As a young volcanic island, its soil layer is very thin which makes the island largely unsuitable for cultivation. Water is quickly lost through the layer of volcanic ash soil, so rice farming is almost impossible. This is one of the reasons the island has also been known as *Samjaedo*/삼재도^{the island of three}

disasters. These refer to Pungjae/풍재/風災 the disaster of wind, Sujae/수재/水災 the disaster of water(floods) and Hanjae/한재/旱災 the disaster of drought.[7]

That being said, the cruelty the islanders suffered at the hands of the climate is nothing compared to the cruelty inflicted upon them by outsiders. Throughout their history, the people of Jeju have been subject both to countless foreign raids and invasions, as well as extended periods of economic exploitation and cultural suppression orchestrated by those in mainland Korea.

It is inevitable then that the many *Shin*/신/神 gods of Jeju are joined by countless *Gwi*/귀/鬼 ghosts formed from the sudden and violent deaths of its inhabitants. Ghosts are the fifth abundance of the island, and they are every bit a part of it as the other four.

What follows is an introduction to these ghosts and gods and the spaces in which they reside. It is accompanied by the fifty-two kinds of cards for the game I have made, but it can be read separately. Brief though it is, I hope that by the end of this book, the reader, like me, can gain an appreciation for the island's distinct pantheon, and through doing so rediscover the magic of the world around us. For even the most ordinary places and objects are inhabited by these spirits: the rooms of a house, the shade under a large tree, even the surface of a single weatherbeaten rock...

Chapter One.
Tomb & Ghost Cards

Sandam
Encroaching Roots
Moving the Grave
Bone Infesting Insects
Weeding the Grave
Resentful Ancestor Spirits
Hanyangilwol
Sumyeongjangja's Household

산담
Sandam

As a country with a long history of ancestor worship, the proper burial of the dead is a matter taken very seriously in Korea. To find evidence of this, one need only take a stroll through the Korean countryside. Wherever you go, you will see the grassy clumps of burial mounds, the shiny black surfaces of headstones and the dignified faces of tomb guardians. Jeju is no exception.

What distinguishes the tombs of Jeju from those on the mainland is their addition of the **Sandam/산담**[tomb wall], which can also refer to the unique Jeju-style tomb itself. The reasons for building Sandam reveal the distinct climate and history of the island:

1. **To stop animals from trampling over the mounds and**

eating the grass growing on their tops. Jeju has been used as pasture land for cows and horses for hundreds of years. If these animals spoil the tombs, this would, of course, anger the ancestors buried within.[8]

2. **To prevent damage from fires used in slash-and-burn agriculture.** This farming technique was necessary in Jeju during the Joseon era(1392-1897), as the lack of steel on the island at that time meant they didn't have the materials to make many farming tools.[9]

3. **To remove and make use of the various volcanic rocks strewn all over the island.**[10]

4. **To shelter the dead from the fierce winds that blow over the island.**[11]

Moreover, Sandam is a wall built to keep things out, not to trap the spirit buried within. The spirit is free to come and go through *Shinmun*/신문/神門 spirit door, a small gap in the wall of the tomb. Shinmun acts as the front gate of the 'house' of the spirit. Sometimes, at the end of this door is a terrace stone that serves as a porch where the spirits can take off their shoes before going into their home. And the long stone placed over Shinmun is called *Jeongdol*/정돌, which serves as a kind of door blocking the entrance to the tomb.[12]

The positioning of Shinmun depends on the gender of the soul within. Traditionally, the right side symbolises feminine yin energy/음기, while the left side symbolises masculine yang energy/양기, so women's graves have Shinmun on the right side and men's on the left.[13]

Sandam is not, however, the only form of protection the island's dead receive. There are two main kinds of statues, which sometimes stand in front of the tomb's burial mound. The first are Inseok/인석 [statues of civil officials]. Their role is to protect the deceased, and as such, they are placed in directions from which evil energies are believed to flow.[14] These statues are a clear analogue to Munseokin/문석인 or Muninseok/문인석, statues of civil

침입하는 뿌리
Encroaching Roots

officials which attend the tombs of the Korean mainland.[15]

The other kind of statue is more peculiar to Jeju, at least in its placement within a tomb. This is *Dongjaseok*/동자석. '*Dongja*/동자' is an antiquated term for a young child in Korean. Accordingly, these statues are the smallest kind found within Sandam and depict either young bachelors or young maidens the latter of which are also known as *Dongnyeo*/동녀. Their role is not to protect but to serve. As such, they are the errand boys (or girls) of the deceased standing facing each other in pairs, like Inseok statutes.[16]

It is essential that the dead be well protected. In traditional Korean belief, if the dead suffer, so will the living. But more than statues or walls, the best defence for a tomb is choosing a good location.

According to the Korean form of *Feng shui*, *Pungsujiri*/풍수지리 wind water earth principles, vital energy flows beneath the earth. It is believed that if someone is buried at a place where this energy has accumulated, the corpse will absorb this wealth of energy, which will then be transferred to their descendants and thereby influence their fortunes.[17] However, the corpse will not last forever. Its influence is believed to last only for the next four or five generations. Beyond this, descendants will be too far removed to have any connection with the deceased.

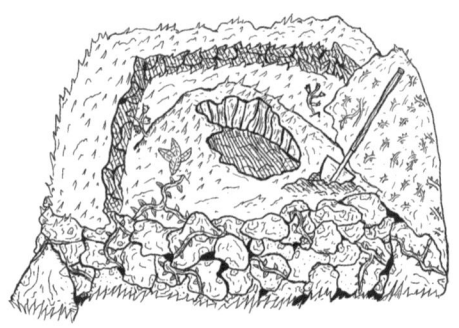

이장
Moving the Grave

Generally speaking, the energy within the bones will last from 50 to 100 years, and when the bones disintegrate entirely, so too will their energy.[18]

Therefore, an auspicious burial site can mean decades of riches and good health while an inauspicious one means decades of suffering. If an ancestor is buried in an area lacking energy or the tomb is neglected, there will be disastrous consequences for that family. One such consequence is disease. During the Joseon Dynasty era(1392-1897), leprosy in particular was considered to be a curse sent by ancestors whose tombs had either been built in the wrong place or **invaded by the roots of surrounding trees**.[19] Therefore, one solution was to move their burial place, called **Ijang/이장** on the mainland and Cheolli/철리 in Jeju.[20] If, after digging up their remains, their bones

뼈에 들끓는 벌레
Bone Infesting Insects

were cracked or had gone yellow you were supposed to clean and reassemble them.

There were even bone-assembling experts who were hired expressly for this task. However, **if the bones were found to be infested with insects,** that was an omen of the end of your family line. People who found this were known to give up on their work and die in poverty and disease.[21]

In Jeju, it is also believed that the bodies of the dead are at risk from a monstrous *Ddang-gwi*/땅귀 [earth ghost] whose name is 'Samdugumi/삼두구미', which literally means 'Three Heads and Nine Tails'. Fortunately, though, he also has three weaknesses: eggs, willow branches and iron. That is why these objects are used to protect the body awaiting reburial during Cheolli/철리 in

Jeju.[22]

However, one need not always go to the trouble of moving the body. The simplest way to protect a tomb from such dangers is '**Beolcho/벌초**'. This literally means 'cutting grass', with the character '벌' coming from the Hanja character, '伐'[cut] and '초' coming from '草'[grass]. As the name suggests, it involves family members tidying up their ancestor's tomb. Traditionally, it is the male descendants who perform this act, trimming the grass on the burial mound with a scythe. This practice takes place either on Hanshik Day/한식/寒食 in the 3rd lunar month, 105 days after Dongji/동지/冬至 [the winter solstice][23] or shortly before Chuseok/추석/秋夕, the Korean harvest thanksgiving festival on the 15th day of the 8th lunar month. In Jeju, the Beolcho takes place on the first day of the 8th lunar month, and such was its importance that up until 2010, it was designated a school holiday.[24]

Though it is long-accepted practice in Korea, Beolcho originates from China. According to legend, it began as a way of commemorating the tragic death of Jie Zhitui, a loyal minister to Duke Wen of Jin:

When the Duke came to power, he forgot to thank Jie for his years of service. Infuriated by this omission, Jie refused to come to court and instead chose to live a life of seclusion with his mother among densely forested moun-

벌초
Weeding the Grave

tains. To flush him out of hiding, the duke ordered his men to start a forest fire. However, the fire soon got out of control and ended up killing both Jie and his mother.

When he found out what his careless actions had cost him, the Duke was devastated. To honour Jie's death, he established the *Qingming* festival, known in English as 'Tomb Sweeping Day[25]' during which people prune the tombs of their ancestors. Yet this festival does not merely placate the resentful soul of Jie. On this day, the spirits of other tragically deceased people are also appeased. In particular, rituals are conducted for the spirits of those who are buried in fields or by the sides of roads.[26]

A similar rite held in Jeju is known as *Ggamagwi Moreun Shik-kei*/까마귀 모른 식게(제사) ancestral rite unknown to crows. Also held in the 3rd lunar month, this is a simple, quiet affair. Only parents and their children attend the rite rather than the entire extended family as is the case with the proper ancestral rite. The name comes from the fact that it is held for spirits who no longer have any descendants. Even the crow, which the natives believed to be capable of travelling between this world and the next, is unaware of their passing. So, these spirits rely on strangers for sustenance. To abandon them is unthinkable. As with other resentful ancestor spirits, they spread disease to the community. Known as *Juksanee*/죽산이,

조상원귀
Resentful Ancestor Spirits

they have died a miserable death; a *Gaeksa*/객사 ^{a death away from home}.[27] They are then a form of *Gaekgwi*/객귀 or *Wongwi*/원귀 ^{resentful spirit/ghost} who because of the uncomfortable or sudden nature of their death, are weighed down by their resentment from moving onto the next life, *Jeoseung*/저승 ^{literally the 'Other World'}.[28] In Jeju, these kinds of spirits are believed to be all too common. This belief reflects the sad harsh reality of life on the island, where many men died at sea or were killed by pirates or the rigours of forced labour.[29]

A kind of ghost prevalent on both Jeju and the mainland was *Songakshee*/손각시^{the spirit of a young, unmarried woman}.[30] This was particularly true during the Joseon Dynasty era. Then, as stipulated by the prevailing Confucian ideology, only the spirits of married women were allowed to receive ancestral rites. Daughters were considered to be temporary members of their birth family and could only be commemorated at the *Sadang*/사당, the ancestral shrine of the family they would marry into. Consequently, if they died before marriage, they were confined to a kind of limbo, unable to join their ancestors in the next life and ignored by their descendants in this life.[31] That was how they became the most feared of all kinds of Wongwi/원귀.

But resentment wasn't the only reason these ghosts

were so dangerous. Their hatred for the living was also driven by unrequited love and unfulfilled lust. Having died before marriage, they were denied any contact with the opposite gender. Accordingly, during their burial, they were exposed to as much male contact as was possible. The bodies of young women were dressed in men's clothes and buried under busy roads, where they would be soothed by the trample of male feet.[32]

Sometimes, however, even these measures were not enough. One particularly tenacious Songakshee/손각시 is featured in the story of the *Go Jeonjeok Josang Bonpuri/* 고전적 조상 본풀이|the unravelling of ancestor Go Jeonjeok's origin.[33] This story revolves around the character of Go Jeonjeok, a civil servant from Jeju. While working in *Hanyang* the name of Seoul during the Joseon dynasty era a young woman known only in the Bonpuri as '**Hanyangilwol/한양일월**seoul ancestor'[34] fell in love with him. But he was already married, and when he had served his time in his post in Seoul, he was only too happy to return home to Jeju. Though Hanyangilwol tried to make him stay, he coldly rejected her advances and chided her for her impudence.

Unfortunately for him, that was not the last he saw of her. She was so distraught by his rejection that she wasted away and, immediately upon her death, turned into a ghost and followed him home. Her spirit got itself into a lady's accessory box and attached to the clothes within. In this form, she floated all the way to the shores of Jeju and was eventually found by Akseangee/악생이, Go Jeonjeok's maid.

Aksaengee's first thought upon seeing what lay within was how beautiful these clothes would look on her mistress. She returned home at once, eager to present this gift to Go Jeonjeok's daughter.

When her mistress wore the clothes within, a terrible change came over her. As she began to admire herself in the mirror, her whole body began to shake and she started to froth at the mouth. She had lost her mind, now possessed by the spirit of Hanyangilwol.

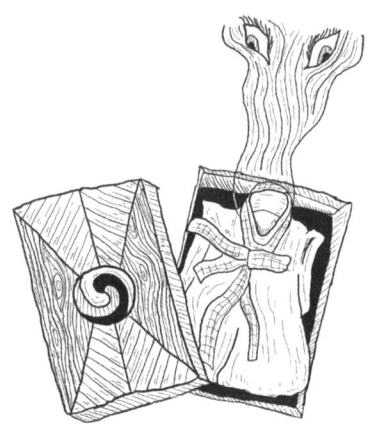

한양일월
Hanyangilwol

When Go Jeonjeok saw his precious daughter in such a state, he sought the advice of a shaman. The shaman quickly identified the cause of her madness and the method with which it might be cured, though this was not to Go Jeonjeok's liking. In the ritual to expel the spirit, he was forced to dance with the possessed body of his daughter, thereby giving Hanyangilwol's spirit a shred of the affection she had yearned for in life.

Yet even that was not enough. Seven days later, Go Jeonjeok's daughter was dead. Devastated with their loss, Go Jeonjeok and his maid died soon afterwards, and when the shaman heard what had happened, their body began to shake and they collapsed to the ground, never to rise again.[35]

According to *Cheonjiwang Bonpuri*/천지왕 본풀이[the unravelling of the king of heaven and earth's origin], Wongwi/원귀 such as Hanyangilwol have plagued the world almost since its creation. As its name suggests, this Bonpuri follows the figure of the Cheonjiwang/천지왕[the king of heaven and earth]. He was the first ruler of the universe, and like all good rulers, he saw that his priority was to bring peace and harmony to those he ruled. To do so, he needed to unite heaven and earth.

So it was that Cheonjiwang, a man of heaven, descended to earth in search of a human wife. What he valued most of all in a woman was not beauty or wealth, but wisdom. Having scoured the land, he found such a woman named Chongmyeong/총명 in a quiet, unassuming village. But when he asked her parents for her hand in marriage, they were embarrassed rather than overjoyed at the proposal. Though they were glad to give their consent, they were ashamed that they couldn't give him much of a dowry. They didn't have enough rice to prepare even a small wedding feast.

That was what led them to the house of **Sumyeongjangja/수명장자**. He was the richest man in the area, perhaps in the whole world. He possessed prodigious strength, which gave him the confidence to stand up to anything, whether it be man, beast or god. Nothing scared him, so he had no fear of punishment. He did whatever he wanted, and what he wanted was to hold power over others. All had to pay him tribute, and this tribute was so costly that those who paid it barely had enough left to survive.

When he found Chongmyeong's parents begging for rice at his door, he treated them the same way he treated everyone. He gave them rice, expensive white rice in fact, but when they got back home, they realised he had mixed it with sand. Unappetising though this was, it was the only food they had, so they tried their best to separate the grains of sand from the grains of rice. They washed it nine times, but of course, this wasn't enough. With his first bite, Cheonjiwang felt the gritty texture of sand.

This was unacceptable. Erupting into anger, he rounded on Chongmyeong's parents, though they were ready with an excuse. It was Sumyeongjangja, not them, who was responsible for such a paltry wedding feast. He, they said, was the cause of so many problems. Hearing this, Cheonjiwang grew interested. He bid them to tell him more about this man, and the more he heard, the angrier he became.

Sumyeongjangja owed his immense wealth not only to terror and intimidation, but also to deception and miserliness. When poor people asked him for rice, he mixed it with white sand, and when they asked him for foxtail millet/조, he mixed it with black sand. When giving, he gave little, but when asking to be repaid, he demanded much in return.

His children were much the same. When his daughters employed labourers to weed their fields, they fed them with rotten soy sauce, keeping all the fresh sauce for themselves. His sons even deceived him. When he asked them to give water to the horses and cows, they left their troughs empty. All they did was give the illusion that the horses had drunk by urinating on their hooves.

At this, Cheonjiwang decided he had heard enough.

Such people, devoid of compassion for both man and beast, were not fit to live. All that they deserved was swift retribution. The agents of this retribution were three of his most fearsome generals: Byeorak Janggun/벼락장군 the lightning general, Oorwe Janggun/우뢰장군 the thunder general and Hwadeok Janggun/화덕장군 the brazier general.

What happened next varies. In some versions, Sumyeongjangja and his entire family were burnt to death, when their house was set ablaze by a hail of lightning bolts. In others, Sumyeongjangja fought to the end, killing many of the soldiers of heaven before he was eventually subdued. Where the various versions of Bonpuri agree is that Sumyeongjangja and his entire family came to a sticky end. Yet even then, they continued to make trouble. They lived on as the first Wongwi/원귀, resentful spirits. In response, shamans held the very first *Gut*/굿 shamanist ritual to exorcise them, and from then on, it became the custom for the resentful souls of people who died in fires to seek out offerings given to them round the back of shrines. It also became the custom to hold Buljjik-Gut/불찍굿 to the Brazier General every time a fire broke out.

Some accounts also mention the various animal reincarnations of Sumyeongjangja's family. These were punishments inflicted on them by Cheonjiwang, each befitting the cruelties they had committed as humans. Sumyeongjangja's daughters, who had denied their servants decent food, were turned into Pat Beolle/팥벌레 red bean bugs(callosobruchus chinensis), which, as their name suggests, feed on stored legumes such as red beans. Meanwhile, Sumyeongjangja's sons, who had given no water to their cattle, were turned into kites. In this form, they are condemned to eternal thirst, with the only water they can consume the rainwater that collects in their feathers.[36]

수명장자의 집
Sumyeongjangja's Household

Chapter Two. Shaman Cards

~~~~~~~~~~~~~~~~~~~~~~~~~~~~~~~~~~~~~~

Shimbang
Yeongjip
Sam-mengdoo

심방
Shimbang

Korean shamans are the Peninsula's foremost experts in expelling resentful spirits. They have been helping ghosts move on to the next life for thousands of years. But exorcist is just one of the many roles they perform. They, like all shamans, are also healers, diviners, bringers of fortune and the officiants of sacrifices.[37]

The shamans of Jeju are known as **Shimbang/심방**. The meaning of this name is open to interpretation. It may denote someone in a trance, someone attached to a god[38], someone who does the errands of a god, or even the child of a god.[39] Alternatively, they are sometimes called Shineui-Seongbang/신의성방 which means the first person in the world to communicate with a god.[40]

Like the shamans of the mainland, the chief tool at the Shimbang's disposal is the *Gut*/굿 or *Kut*. This is a complex shamanist ritual consisting of various elements. Song, dance, and dramatic recitations are all performed to call down blessings from the gods and expel harmful ghosts.[41] Gut can also guarantee the safe passage of the dead into the next life and enable the bereaved to say their final goodbyes.

A core component of the Gut is the *Bonpuri*/본풀이. *Bon*/본 means origin(本), and *Puri*/풀이 means solution or unravelling. Therefore, Bonpuri refers to the story of the origin of a god.[42] The Bonpuri plays the most important role in Jeju Gut. It sheds light on how the god rose to its current status and how it came to be worshipped. The Shimbang, by reciting the Bonpuri, entertains and flatters the god, thereby making it more likely that they will grant the requested favour.[43]

The literal tools used by Shimbang also play a critical role in their initiation and the performance of rituals. These tools are called *Kimae*/기메. One interesting example of a paper type of Kimae is the **Yeongjip/영집**, which literally means 'Soul House'. As the name suggests, the Yeongjip is a place of rest and comfort for lost souls. It is commonly used in a kind of Gut known as the Muhon-Gut/무혼굿. This Gut is performed on the behalf of all those who have drowned at sea, and its purpose is to send them off safely to the afterlife. Because of the nature of their death, these souls had no one to give them a proper burial, and so they were filled with resentment.

During this Gut, a doll representing the deceased is dressed in their clothes and covered in a blanket and folding screen. The Yeongjip is then placed atop a scattering of buckwheat or rice powder. With the necessary Kimae tools and offerings prepared, the Shimbang prays that the deceased move on from their previous life and

영집
Yeongjip

삼멩두
Sam-mengdoo

be reincarnated. When the Gut is finished, the Yeongjip is cleared away, and the Shimbang inspects the powder within. If the soul that took refuge within has reincarnated as a bird, then a symbol like a bird's foot will appear in the powder, and if they have turned into a butterfly, a symbol resembling a butterfly's wings will appear.[44]

The most frequently used set of Kimae tools is the *Sam-mengdoo*/삼멩두. This name refers to the following three sets of objects:

Shinkal/신칼: A kind of sacred knife also referred to as the Shi-wang Daebeonji/시왕대번지.

Sanpan/산판: A set of several objects, including a pair of Cheonmun/천문^{heavenly gates}, brass discs resembling coins with three Chinese characters, 天 ^{heaven}, 地 ^{earth}, and 門 ^{gate} engraved upon them; a pair of small brass cups resembling those alcohol is drunk out of known as Sangjan/상잔, and lastly, a brass dish known as Sandae/산대 used for storing the Cheonmun and Sangjan.

Yoryang/요량: A small brass bell which is attached to various pieces of multicoloured cloth.[45]

This set of Kimae is treated with the utmost respect, for they embody the shaman ancestor gods of Jeju, three brothers named Bonmyeongdu/본명두, Shinmyeongdu/신명두, and Sammyeongdu/삼명두.[46] These Kimae tools are also sometimes referred to simply as Josang/조상^{ancestor}. They are handed down from shaman to shaman, and so the souls of the shamans who used them before are also believed to inhabit the objects.

Chapter Three.
Confucian Magistrate Cards

~~~~~~~~~~~~~~~~~~~~~~~~

Magistrate Lee Hyeongsang
Magistrate Yang
Cheongu-agoo-daemeng-ee

이형상 목사
Magistrate Lee Hyeongsang

In spite of the important roles they play, shamans have not always been valued by Korean society. During the time of the Joseon Dynasty era(1392-1897), shamans were relegated to the lowest caste in society: Cheonmin/ 천민vulgar people. Espousing a strict adherence to rationalist Neo-Confucian ideals, Joseon monarchs denigrated shamans as swindlers, infecting the commoners with their vulgar superstitions. Though during the previous Goryeo Dynasty(918-1392), shamans had been excluded from the government and state affairs[47], during the Joseon dynasty era, shamans became excluded even from villages. They, alongside other so-called Cheonmin such as butchers and blacksmiths, were forced to live in isolated areas some way away from the village.⁴⁸

Such isolation was deemed necessary as shamans were seen as a serious threat to the state religion. According to Confucian thought, rulers alone were bestowed with the Mandate of Heaven. They were both monarchs and high priests, offering sacrifices to spirits at official altars to ensure the prosperity of the whole country. Aside from the king, various Confucian officials were also tasked with making contact with the spirit world and performing certain ceremonies. Shamans, however, undermined this hierarchy. They went around the king and his officials, directly contacting the spirits, sometimes even using their own bodies as altars.⁴⁹

As the farthest flung province of Joseon, Jeju and its shamans remained for many years largely unregulated and undisturbed by the state's ruling ideology.

This all changed in 1702 with the appointment of **'Lee Hyeongsang/이형상'** as the Island's new Moksa/목사 ᶜᵒᵘⁿᵗʸ ᵐᵃᵍⁱˢᵗʳᵃᵗᵉ. He was determined to spread Confucianism and bring order to the Island's religious beliefs. To him, many of the Island's religious ceremonies fell under the category of Eumsa/음사ⁱᵐᵐᵒʳᵃˡ ʳⁱᵗᵘᵃˡˢ⁵⁰, ⁵¹, or more technically, rituals not included in the Joseon manual for rituals- the Sajeon/사전/祀典 ʳⁱᵗᵘᵃˡ ˡᵃʷ.⁵²

He had no tolerance for these breaches of the law.

In his campaign to rid the island of Eumsa, he laid waste to at least 129 shrines, as well as several Buddhist temples.[53]

However, he wouldn't have much time to celebrate his victory. The political faction he was a member of fell out of favour at court, and in 1703, he was dismissed from office.[54] His replacement, Lee Hwitae/이희태, then proceeded to undo all that he had accomplished. Immediately after arriving in Jeju, Lee Hwitae held a grand ritual for the gods of Jeju and commanded the Shimbang to rebuild the shrines that had been destroyed.[55]

But though his tenure as Moksa was short, Lee Hyeongsang certainly left a mark upon the Island. Various legends describe his confrontations with different gods. One such god was the 'Gwangjeongdangshin/광정당신'. According to oral tradition, this god took the form of a great serpent, and when Lee saw it emerging from its shrine in Andeokmyeon/안덕면, he had his soldiers slay it on the spot.[56]

Confrontations between shamanist snakes and Confucian men were not confined to Jeju either. The *Tosan Bonpuri*/토산본풀이[57], begins with one such standoff in the county of Naju/나주 in southwest Korea.

Long ago, each time a magistrate was appointed to the county of Naju, they died the very day they arrived. Understandably, it soon became impossible to find an-

양씨 목사
Magistrate Yang

yone willing to take the position. At last, though, one fearless man, '**Yang-shee/양씨**^{Mr. Yang}', accepted the summons. He set off at once, but as he entered the region and passed by the Geumseongsan/금성산^{Geumseong Mountain}, his accompanying attendants grew nervous and urged him to dismount from his horse. They feared that if he remained on horseback, he would upset the spirit of the mountain who looked after the surrounding villages. However, Yang-shee would not submit to such superstition and instead rode up the mountain, cajoling his terrified retinue to follow behind.

Some way up the mountain, they came across a house with a blue-tile roof. Yang-shee dismounted and then walked into the inner courtyard, where he was greeted by a beautiful woman. He was not taken in by her charms, though, and called out to her: "Are you a person or a ghost?" But before she could respond, he demanded that she show him her true form.

What followed was a monstrous transformation. In place of the woman, there was now a colossal serpent, so large that its top jaw rested on the heavens and its bottom jaw lay on the earth. This was the true form of the spirit-the **Cheongu-agoo-daemeng-ee/천구아구대멩이**. Horrified by this vision, Yang-shee's servants screamed and began to scatter. Yang-shee remained calm though and called out for his long sword. As soon as it was handed to him, he fearlessly decapitated the beast. He then had his men set its house on fire, and in an instant, it was reduced to ashes.[58]

천구아구대멩이
Cheongu-agoo-daemeng-ee

Chapter Four.
Snake God Cards

~~~~~~~~~~~~~~~~~~~~

Chilseong-shinsang and Heomeng-ee doll
Bangool Poom
Anchilseong
Gopang

칠성신상과 허멩이 인형
Chilseong-shinsang and Heomeng-ee doll

Snakes have been the object of worship in Jeju for hundreds of years. A scholar, Kim Jeong/김정, wrote a book in Jeju while he was exiled to the Island in 1520 called *Jeju Pungtorok*/제주풍토록 record of the climate of Jeju. In this he mentioned how the Island was infested with snakes due to its high humidity. He also mentioned that the locals didn't see this as a curse but rather as a blessing. Whenever they saw a snake, instead of chasing it away, they recited a prayer and offered it alcohol.[59] Furthermore, unlike other wild, dangerous animals, snakes actually chose to live alongside the islanders, taking shelter under their fences, in their walls, or even in the thatch of their roofs. Thus, instead of just fear, the islanders also felt an affinity with these cohabiting creatures.[60]

So, it goes without saying that the islanders never dared to kill a snake. In Jeju's folklore, it is said that even seeing a dead snake can cause blindness. Therefore, you should at once cover your eyes and look away. Worse still, if you touch the dead snake, your hand will rot away. The spirit of the dead snake is both furious and confused. Therefore, it may easily mistake you as its killer and curse you in revenge. The symptoms of this curse are as follows: your tongue will dart in and out like a snake, your skin will become scaly like a snake, and the part of you that touched the snake will ache painfully.

The only cure is to hold the ritual known as the *Chilseong-saenam-Gut*/칠성새남굿. A critical component of this Gut is the *Heomeng-ee Nollim*/허멩이 놀림 teasing the Heomeng-ee. This ritual involves the creation of the '**Heomeng-ee doll/허멩이 인형**', which represents the actual murderer of the snake. Though it resembles a man of *Yangban*/양반noble status, it is, in fact, an arrogant, harmful spirit, which aside from killing snakes also delights in starting fires and spreading all other kinds of disaster.

In the Heomeng-ee Nollim, the shaman acts as a judge and has the doll lie flat on the ground where it is flogged and a 'confession' is forced out of it. The spirit within is banished to *Gakdagwi-Island*/각다귀섬. Gakdagwi has a double meaning. It refers both to insects like mosquitoes which drink the blood of other animals, and people who live off and exploit the hard work of others.

To make sure that the snake witnesses the confession, it, like the Heomeng-ee, is made manifest in the form of a paper doll, this time resembling a snake. This is known as the '**Chilseong-shinsang/칠성신상**seven star god image'. Confident that it has been avenged, the snake is ready to be reborn. From then on, the spirit of the snake no longer harbours resentment, and so the unfortunate witness to its death is released from its curse.[61]

The name of the doll may initially appear to be at odds with its purpose and appearance. However, in Jeju mythology, the seven stars of the Big Dipper, known as the 'Chilseongshin/칠성신' in Korean, are intimately connected with the island's snake gods. The Chilseongshin have been worshipped in Korea for thousands of years and are believed to control the destinies of all mankind.[62] Each of the seven Chilseongshin influences our lives in a unique way. For example, one is in charge of distributing disasters, and another responsible for setting our lifespans.[63] As we shall soon see, this parallels the way in which each of the island's snake gods protect a different house or region. One of these snake gods we will encounter soon even shares the name of the Chilseongshin. With this in mind, it makes perfect sense that a representation of a snake be called the Chilseong-shinsang.

Returning to the ritual of the Heomeng-ee Nollim, when the snake sees the Heomeng-ee confess and be punished, it is then ready to move on from its resentment.

Another way to remove a dead snake's curse is the ritual of '**Bangool Poom/방울품**^{untying the bells}'. It began as a means to soothe the spirit of a snake which suffered not one but two violent deaths. We have already encountered the first death: decapitation at the hands of Yang-shee, the magistrate dispatched to the county of Naju.

Although he would never know it, Yang-shee had not killed the creature. It lived on in a different form.

As the corpse of the great serpent fell to earth, it turned into a shower of gold and jade stones. These rained down on the city of Seoul, scattering across the Jongno/종로 crossroads. There, they caught the eyes of three men from Jeju: Mr. Gang/강씨, Mr. O/오씨, and Mr. Han/한씨. These three had journeyed to the capital to pay tribute to the king, offering up the specialties of Jeju

방울품
Bangool Poom

such as clams and seaweed. Pocketing a few of the stones each, they set off for the palace. Unbeknownst to them, the stones were imbued with magic and it was thanks to this, that they were able to deliver the tribute without any problems.

On the way back home though, the men lost interest in the stones and ended up throwing them away. This was a mistake. When they finally reached a port, their ship was blown back by powerful winds and they could barely even leave the harbour. At a loss of what else to do, they sought out a renowned shaman. He or she[64] told them that they still carried one of the stones and in order to go home, they first needed to hold a Gut in its honour. Then and only then would the winds change.

The three men did as they were told, and sure enough soon after the Gut was completed, a southerly wind came to their rescue and carried their ship all the way back to Jeju. It was by no means an uneventful journey back home though, as when the ship came into harbour, the remaining stone took on the form of a beautiful young woman, an *Agishee*/아기씨. But before anyone could call out to her or even grasp what was happening, the woman disembarked and was gone.

Going ashore, the Agishee made herself at home. Following the advice of a local god, she enshrined herself as the village god of Tosan-li/토산리 on the Island's southeastern coastline. Yet far though it was from the site of her first 'death', it was no less dangerous. One day while she and her handmaiden were washing clothes in a spring by the sea, they were attacked and killed by Japanese pirates.

Sometime later, the locals found the bodies of the two women and buried them in twin tombs to placate their resentful spirits. However, this was not enough. The Agishee demanded worship, and when she didn't get it, she lashed out at the other young women of the community. Some women lost their lives as Japanese pirate attacks continued, and others lost control of their bodies, possessed by the spirit of the Agishee.

Eventually, as they always did in times of spiritual crisis, the locals turned to the local Shimbang. He or she[65], with the help of the possessed girls, discovered the cause of the recent misfortunes and so was born the ritual of 'Bangool Poom'. To unravel the resentment of Agishee, the Shimbang drew the likeness of a snake onto paper and tied up knots of silk resembling bells. These the Shimbang placed on the bodies of the afflicted girls. They then unwound the knots and through doing so, also resolved the grudge of the Bangool Agishee/방울아기씨[lady of the bells] as the spirit was then known. The girls were freed from possession and a new cure was discovered. Soon the ritual spread all across the Island.[66]

Freed from resentment, the Agishee became the kindly deity she had always intended to be. She now protected the young women she had once harmed, no matter where they were. When the local women married, they took the worship of the spirit with them. They built small cave-like structures out of straw, known as *Chilseongnul*/칠성눌 in their yards to serve as her sanctuary.[67]

It is a mark of the Islanders' deep respect for snakes that Bangool Agishee is not the only snake god worshipped within the home. She is accompanied by another god, **Anchilseong/안칠성**the inner seven star god. These two gods have much in common. Not only do they share the same form and home, they also share a similarly traumatic origin story.

The Anchilseong was originally an *Agashee*/아가씨a nobleman's unmarried daughter from China. At a young age, she

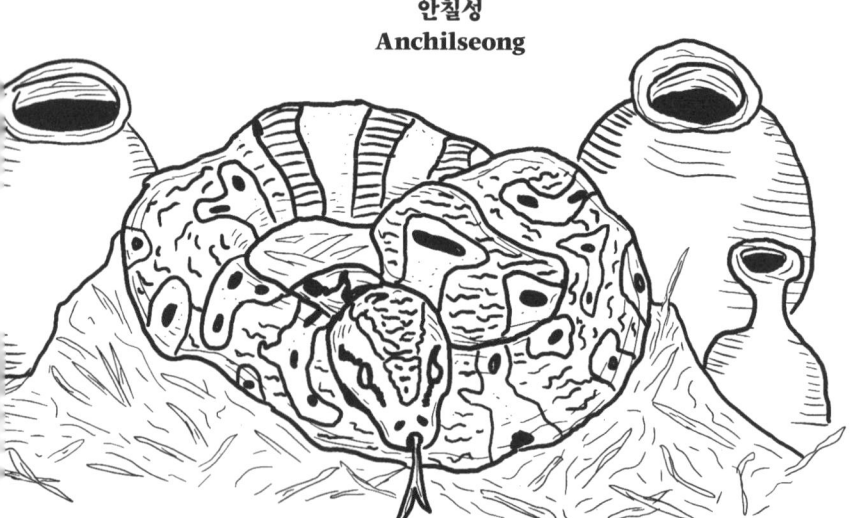

안칠성
Anchilseong

was abducted by a Buddhist monk, and when she finally returned home, her parents were horrified to see that she had fallen pregnant. As a wealthy noble family, they could not bear the scandal this would cause, so they cast her out of the family home for good. They shut her in an iron box and threw it into the eastern sea.

This box (somehow) floated across the ocean and eventually washed up on the shores of Jeju. Miraculously, she had not only survived but had also given birth to seven healthy children. However, the journey had taken its toll. Both she and her children had transformed into snakes.

Slithering around Jeju, they, like the Agishee of the Tosan Bonpuri, searched for followers. The first person to see them as more than just snakes was a woman named Songdaejeong Buin/송대정부인^{wife of Song Daejeong}. Thinking they might be some kind of *Josangshin*/조상신 ^{ancestor spirit}, she carefully carried them back to her house and enshrined them within the *Gopang*/고팡^{storeroom} of her house.

Sometime later, the mother snake called all her daughters together. She told them that they could no longer all live in one place, as the offerings would eventually run out. She asked each of her daughters where they would enshrine themselves, and so it was that the various jurisdictions of the snake gods were decided:

The eldest daughter said she would occupy a pond within Jeju city.

The second daughter said she would occupy the local government offices.

The third daughter said she would occupy the prison.

The fourth daughter said she would occupy the orchards in the east and west.

The fifth daughter said she would occupy the storerooms in the east and west.

The sixth said she would also occupy another pond within Jeju city.

❼

The seventh, most filial daughter said she would occupy the tangerine tree in the back garden and would offer the tangerines to her mother in thanks.

The Mother then declared that she would take care of the storeroom in the house the **Gopang/고팡** and look after the crops within. Thereafter, she would be called Anchilseong/안칠성^{the inner seven star god}.⁶⁸ This name is most likely a reference to her role as guardian. As we have seen already, the Chilseongshin/칠성신 are the deified seven stars of the Big Dipper, which is called 'Bukduchilseong/북두칠성' in Korean. They are the masters of human destiny. Anchilseong of Jeju is then the Chilseongshin in miniature. While the Chilseongshin preside over the fortunes of all humanity, Anchilseong presides over the fortunes of a single household.

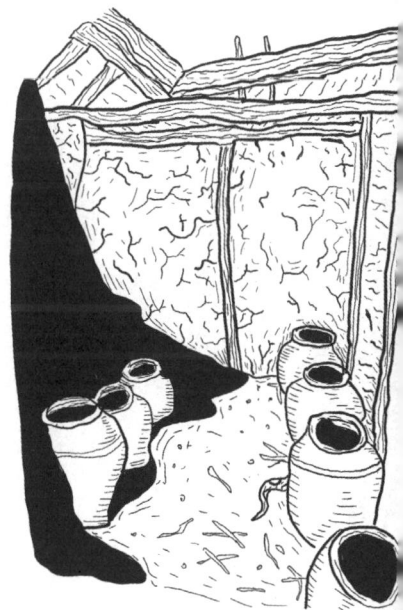

고팡
Gopang

Chapter Five.
Household God Cards

Jumokjishin
Jeongjumok and Jeongnang
Noiljedaegwi-il's Daughter
Jeongji
Jowang Halmang
Munjeonshin
Sangbang
Haunted House

주목지신
Jumokjishin

Snakes are far from the only gods inhabiting the traditional Jeju home. A whole host of gods are crammed into its every nook and cranny. The majority of these *Gashin*/가신^{household gods} as they are known, are featured in the *Munjeon-Bonpuri*/문전본풀이.

This Bonpuri tells the story of Nam Seonbi/남선비^{scholar Nam}, his wife Yeosan Buin/여산부인^{lady Yeosan} and their seven sons. They were a poor but happy family. Trouble only entered their lives when the family expanded to include a new member, '**Noiljedaegwi-il's Daughter/노일제대귀일의 딸**'.

This woman was renowned for her cunning and

greed. When Nam Seonbi travelled to her home of Odong Country/오동나라 to sell rice, she tricked him into gambling away all his money. Then, with no way to return home, the destitute Nam Seonbi was forced to marry her. Though now he had no more money left for her to steal, she began to sap his energy instead. Every day, she fed him on nothing but rice-bran gruel, and he soon went blind.

Three years later, his concerned first wife, Yeosan Buin, went looking for him. But though she did manage to find him, their long-awaited reunion was cut short. Noiljedaegwi-il's Daughter refused to stand aside. She tricked Yeosan Buin into wading into a river, the Jucheon-gang/주천강^{Jucheon River} and then pushed her into its deepest part and drowned her. With Yeosan Buin dead, Noiljedaegwi-il's Daughter assumed her identity. When she returned to Nam Seonbi, she mimicked his beloved first wife's voice and told him how she had killed Noiljedaegwi-il's Daughter. Nam Seonbi was overjoyed at this news and suggested that they return home to 'their' sons.

This, of course, would present great difficulties for their 'mother'. Nam Seonbi's sons were not so easily fooled as their father. When their 'parents' finally returned home, the brothers were bemused by their mother's sudden change in appearance. When they remarked on this, their supposed mother told them it was merely a result of how much she had suffered while searching for their father.

It wasn't a very convincing excuse, and she knew it. Realising that she would soon be uncovered, she decided to strike first. She feigned illness and told Nam Seonbi that the only cure was to eat the seven livers of 'her' sons.

Fortunately, the sons overheard her, and the youngest brother Nokdiseongin/녹디성인 came up with a ploy of his own. He cut out the livers of six piglets and, claiming that they were the livers of his six brothers, offered them up to Noiljedaegwi-il's Daughter. However, even she wasn't so monstrous as to actually eat the livers. She told Nokdiseongin to leave her so she could eat them in peace, and then when he was gone, she merely pretended to eat them and hid them under her blanket. Nokdiseongin had seen all this though, as he had been watching her secretly. When she told him that she needed to eat just one more liver to be cured, he could contain his rage no longer. Snatching the livers from under her blanket, he climbed onto the roof of his house and called out to all their neighbours, telling them all about how this woman had disguised herself as his mother and tried to kill him and his brothers.

Soon enough, the entire neighbourhood had heard, and an angry mob descended upon the house. The thunderous rush of the crowds outside shook both Nam Seonbi and Noiljedaegwi-il's Daughter to the core. Terrified by what they would do to her, Noiljedaegwi-il's Daughter took her fate into her own hands. She ran into the outhouse and hung herself with her own hair. Nam Seonbi was also seized by panic, consumed by guilt for having almost killed his own sons, and ran down the Olle/올레^{the narrow alley leading to houses in Jeju}. He crashed into the '**Jeongjumok/정주목**^{gateposts}' and died with his neck caught in the '**Jeongnang/정낭**^{wooden cross beams}'. His spirit was also stuck in that place, becoming the protector of the gate, the '**Jumokjishin/주목지신**^{the gatepost earth god}'.

정주목과 정낭
Jeongjumok and Jeongnang

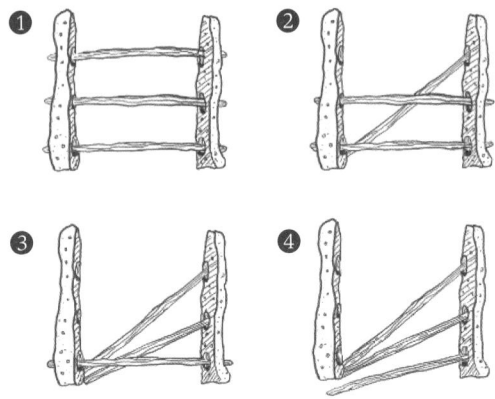

Though he has lost his human body, Nam Seonbi still speaks. The holes of the Jeongjumok are his mouth, and the Jeongnang are his teeth. Therefore, even now his voice is still heard and understood by the islanders. By this, I mean that the placement of the Jeongnang in the Jeongjumok are capable of communication. They have four things to say:

❶ If all three are in the holes, it means the owner will be gone for the whole day.[69]

❷ If the first two are in the holes, it means the owner will be gone for around half a day.

❸ If only the lowest of the Jeongnang is stuck in the holes of the Jeongjumok, it means the owner has gone somewhere close like a neighbour's house, and will be back soon.

❹ If none of the Jeongnang cross beams are in the holes of the Jeongjumok, it means the owner is at home.

*The Names and Positions of the Jeongnang and Jeongjumok: According to Jin Seonggi(진성기), the origins of the two words are as follows:

Jeongnang: Jeong/정 comes from the word for 'lock' in Jeju's dialect, and the Nang/낭 means 'tree' or 'wood' as in Poknang/폭낭[hackberry tree].

Jeongjumok: Jeong/정 has the same origin as above, and Jumok/주목 originates from Jumeok/주먹[pillar].[70]

The spirit of Noiljedaegwi-il's Daughter also became a household god, though first she would endure a gruesome transformation. By forcing her to kill herself, the seven brothers had, in one way, already gotten their revenge. But, suspecting that she had killed their mother, they decided to take revenge a second time, this time on her corpse. They tore apart her legs and, in their place, attached slabs from the floor of the outhouse. They cut off her head and replaced it with a pig trough. They pulled out her hair and threw it into the sea whereupon it transformed into seaweed. Her mouth they sliced off and also cast into the ocean whereupon it transformed into a Solchi/솔치^{a kind of small, sardine-like fish}. The ocean was also the final resting place for her fingers and toes, which turned into different kinds of shellfish. Her entire body was mutilated and metaphorised; her discarded belly button became a cicada lava, and her anus turned into various kinds of clams. The remains of her body were then worn down by the wind and turned into clouds of gnats and mosquitoes. That was how Noiljedaegwi-il's Daughter became Cheukdo Buin/측도부인^{the goddess of the outhouse}.

With their revenge complete, the seven brothers began their journey to find and revive their mother. Their first stop was the *Seocheongotbat*/서천꽃밭, the mythic 'Western Heaven Flower Fields' where they picked

노일제대귀일의 딸
Noiljedaegwi-il's Daughter

조왕할망
Jowang Halmang

the flowers of reincarnation. Next, they tracked down the body of their mother. After a successful prayer to Haneulnim/하늘님^{god of heaven} to dry up the waters of the Jucheon-gang^{Jucheon River} where she had drowned, they scattered the flowers over her remains. It did not take long for the flowers to do their work. Though she had been a mere skeleton a moment before, their mother arose from the lakebed, a woman of flesh and blood once more.

정지
Jeongji

The seven brothers helped her to her feet and warmed her with their embrace. They reassured her that though she had spent a year at the bottom of a freezing lake, she would now forever bask in the warmth of the hearth, for she would become **Jowang Halmang/조왕할망**, the goddess of the kitchen(**Jeongji/정지** as it is known in Jeju dialect).

It is fitting that she be made goddess of the kitchen as she is then as far as possible from her rival in the outhouse. In Jeju, there is the proverb: *Tongshee-wa Jowangeun meolsurok jotda*/통시와 조왕은 멀수록 좋다, which means 'The further the kitchen is from the outhouse, the better.' Therefore, the conflict between the two wives and their desire to keep away from one another is a metaphor for proper hygiene.[71]

The word used here for outhouse, Tongshee moreover refers to the distinctive toilet-cum-pigpen found only on Jeju. The black pigs of Jeju, the Heukdwaeji/흑돼지 were raised in small enclosures to the rear of the house. Attached to this enclosure though was a toilet, so that human waste fell into the pen below and provided some form of sustenance to the poor animals within. Thus, given her association with all kinds of toilet, Noiljedaegwi-il's Daughter is also referred to as the 'Tongshee Halmang/통시할망'.[72]

The conflict between the two wives is also something the women of Jeju would have understood all too well. As mentioned before, Jeju is known as Samdaseom, an island of three bounties: rocks, wind and women. While the first two are products of its climate, the third is a product of its unfortunate history. So many men died

문전신
Munjeonshin

either at sea fishing or through forced labour so that, according to some accounts, there were twice as many women as men. For that reason, many men had multiple wives. According to one magistrate in late Joseon, even very weak men in Jeju had two or three wives, and some men had as many as a dozen.[73]

The *Munjeon Bonpuri*/문전본풀이 concludes with the brothers' own ascension to godhood. They all became the guardians of the traditional Jeju home's various gates. The clever, youngest brother became **Munjeonshin/문전신**, the guardian god of the *Munjeon*/문전 the main gate. This gate stands in front of the middle of the traditional Jeju house, the **Sangbang/상**

상방
Sangbang

방. It is the hub of the house. Known on the mainland as Maru/마루, this raised wooden platform functions as a living room. On either side are bedrooms, kitchens and *Gopang*/고팡^{storeroom}.[74]

As the last two chapters have made clear, the traditional home of the Islanders is every bit as well defended as their tombs. This is just as well for they are both vulnerable to the same dangers. One such danger is invasive plant life. In the Joseon era, it was believed that if trees or other plants grew too close to a house, it would cause great misfortune for its occupants. This was because it facilitated the invasion of malicious, ghostly beings. These included Dok-gak/독각, a lustful spirit which hops around on one leg. Dok-gak would try to seduce the woman of the home and if spurned, take revenge by driving a wooden stake into a field. This would then corrupt the surrounding area so that no crops would grow.[75]

A tree growing within a house was even more inauspicious. This can be seen in the Korean language itself, or rather in Hanja. The words for Poverty(빈곤), Fatigue(피곤), Trouble/Difficulty(곤경/곤란) all include the 곤 character (pronounced 'gon'). Its Hanja character is as follows: 困, which resembles the character for tree(木) within the character for mouth(口).[76] Therefore, an overgrown house with a tree growing within it is almost certainly a **Hyungga/흉가**^{haunted house}.

흉가
Haunted House

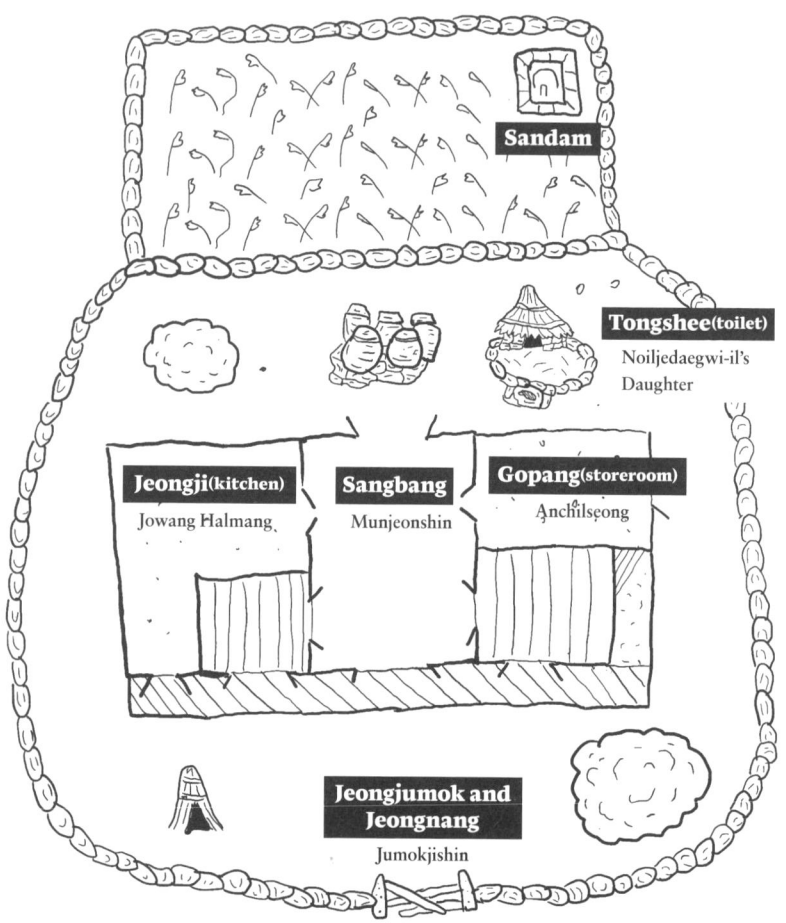

Chapter Six. Death God Cards

~~~~~~~~~~~~~~~~~~

Skull of Samanee's Ancestor
Ganglim
Gwayangsaengee Couple

사만이 조상의 해골
Skull of Samanee's Ancestor

Another kind of god dwelling within the home is the *Josangshin*/조상신^{ancestor god}. The most generous of these gods is perhaps the ancestor of the man Samanee/사만이 in the *Myeonggam Bonpuri*/명감본풀이(or *Menggam Bonpuri*/멩감 본풀이).

Though blessed with a loving family, Samanee lacked the means to support them. He tried his hand at hunting but to no avail. No matter how long he spent roaming the mountains, he failed to catch even a single deer. All that he did find was a single human skull. Or rather, the skull found him. He tried to get away from it, but each time he took a step, the skull was in front of him once again. Eventually, he realised that his discovery of the skull was no coincidence. There must be some kind of connection between him and it. Thinking perhaps that it was the skull of a lost ancestor, he took it home and enshrined it in his storeroom. From then on, each time he held a *Jesa*/제사^{ancestral rite}, he first offered food not to the spirit tablets of his parents but to the skull.

These offerings were not in vain. From that time on, his fortunes began to change. Each time he went out hunting, he caught not one but several deer. The deer flocked to him, attracted by some kind of magnetism. Accordingly, Samanee quickly went from being the poorest man in his village to the richest.

But though his financial troubles were at an end, a far greater threat was lying ahead. One night, while he and his wife were sleeping, the figure of a white-haired old man emerged from the storeroom and woke the couple. He told them how Samanee was in grave danger. Yeomla/염라^{the king of the Otherworld} had dispatched three *Chasal*/차사^{officials sent to arrest criminals} to seize Samanee and carry him off to his realm. But all hope was not lost quite yet. The white-haired spirit told them that this fate was not inevitable. To prevent Samanee's capture, they should go to the place in front of their house where three paths cross. There, they should set up a folding screen and a table filled to the brim with food, decked out as if for a

Jesa. Next, they should write Samanee's name under the table, and when the Chasas saw this and called out, Samanee should reply.

Samanee and his wife did all that they were told. When the Chasas saw the table they had prepared, they began tucking in immediately. Only as they were finishing, did one of them look under the table and see the name 'Samanee' written there: the very man they had been sent to collect. This caused great concern as they realised that they had eaten someone else's food for free, a crime punishable by hanging. To check if it really was his food, they each called out his name, and to their horror, each time they heard his reply. Not knowing what else to do, they pressed onto Samanee's house. There, they found yet more food; food that had actually been prepared for them. Wracked with guilt and moved by his incredible hospitality, they decided that they could not, in good conscience, rob such a man of his life.

They returned to the Otherworld and sneaked into the hall where the lifespans of all living beings are recorded. Somehow, among the countless scrolls, they found Samanee's entry. It had been no mistake to collect the soul of such a young man as it was written that he was destined to live only thirty years. This information, like the records of the Joseon era, was written in Hanja. This was a great stroke of fortune, for it meant it could be changed very easily. With just a single flick of a brush, the Chasas changed the number 'thirty/三十' to 'three thousand/三千'. Later, when Yeomla returned and demanded why Samanee was still among the living, they merely showed him this record, and he realised he had been mistaken.

And so it was that Samanee lived to the ripe old age of three thousand[77] all thanks to the kindness he showed to one lost skull - the Skull of **Samanee's Ancestor/사만이 조상의 해골**.[78]

강림
Ganglim

While the Myeonggam Bonpuri gives valuable advice to us in this world(*Eeseung*/이승), the *Chasa Bonpuri*/차사본풀이 informs us of what lies ahead in the Otherworld(*Jeoseung*/저승). As the name suggests, it explains the origin of one of Chasas, a man named '**Ganglim/강림**'.

Though famous in modern Korea and dreaded in premodern Korea, Ganglim was once like Samanee, a mortal man down on his luck. He was a lowly civil servant tasked with a seemingly impossible assignment. The three sons of the '**Gwayangsaengee Couple/과양생이 부부**' had all died mysteriously. Though they had been perfectly healthy one moment, they were dead the next. The local magistrate, Kimchi Wonnim/김치원님, was unable to resolve the case himself, so he dispatched poor Ganglim to summon the only person who could know what had happened, the only person who knew the causes of all deaths: Great King Yeomla/염라대왕 the king of the otherworld himself.

Ganglim was not alone, however. Despite his many infidelities, he was blessed with the undying love and dedication of his wife. When she heard of his mission, she sprang into action at once, preparing several essential objects. These included several Siruddeok/시루떡 a kind of layered rice cake which she offered up to the house's Jowang Halmang and Munjeonshin. In return, the two spirits guided Ganglim to the Otherworld, and that was how he was able to find Yeomla.

But it was up to Ganglim alone to compel Yeomla to come to the world of the living. This he achieved through a daring ambush. Waiting by the Gate of the

Otherworld, when he saw Yeomla's palanquin passing by, he let out a roar like a clap of thunder and charged. He ripped open its curtains and found the terrified Lord of the Dead quivering inside, completely abandoned by his attendants, who had scattered in all directions. In an instant, Ganglim had bound him with rope (or, in some variants, a chain) so tightly that he could barely breathe.

과양생이 부부
Gwayangsaengee Couple

In that state, Yeomla could do nothing but agree to whatever Ganglim asked of him. That was how Ganglim completed his assignment. At Ganglim's behest, Yeomla appeared before Kimchi Wonnim and the Gwayangsaengee Couple and started unravelling the mystery of their sons' deaths.

The three boys, he revealed, had actually suffered two deaths. Their first death was at the hands of the Gwayangsaengee Couple themselves. Long ago, when the boys had stopped by their house, seeking food and shelter, the couple had robbed and murdered them. They then disposed of their bodies in a pond, and from their bodies had grown three beautiful flowers. Gwayangsaengee's wife had later accidentally swallowed the three flowers and then fallen pregnant. When she gave birth to triplets, she was the happiest she had ever been. Little did she know that her mother's love would be used against her. Fate conspired so that the boys' deaths would be as devastating as possible. They died just after they had passed the civil service exam, the highest aspiration of every man in the Joseon Dynasty era.

But to Yeomla, the anguish Gwayangsaengee and his wife had felt at that moment was not punishment enough. He ordered that the pair of them be killed in the most gruesome way possible. Husband and wife were each tied to nine different cows, which were made to run in different directions. Yet even when the bodies were split into nine different pieces, Yeomla was not satisfied. Their crimes warranted nothing less than almost total annihilation. He assembled the young women of the area at a mill to ground their remains into a fine powder.

This, he then blew into the wind, whereupon it changed into a cloud of gnats and mosquitoes that flew away in all directions.

Even after all this, Yeomla wasn't finished. He had been greatly impressed by Ganglim. Though a mere mortal, he had travelled between worlds and though he had received a lot of help, he had undoubtedly shown great courage. With this in mind, Yeomla asked Kimchi Wonnim if he would let Ganglim work for him instead. When Kimchi Wonnim refused, wily old Yeomla came up with a compromise: Kimchi Wonnim could hold onto Ganglim's body while Yeomla took his soul. To this, Kimchi Wonnim foolishly agreed. Therefore, with no one asking for his views on the matter, poor Ganglim's soul was plucked from his body and dragged to the Otherworld by Yeomla. That was how he became the *Jeoseung Saja*/ 서승사자 the spirit who escorts the souls of the dead to the Otherworld.

Meanwhile, Kimchi Wonnim, thinking he had gotten the better end of the deal, began ordering Ganglim's body to do this and that. However, these orders fell on deaf ears. The soulless husk of the body merely stood there motionless.[79]

Chapter Seven. Village God Cards

Socheonguk
Sanshin Baekgwan of Gonaebong
Bangsatap
Dolhareubang

소천국
Socheonguk

Household Gods are not the only gods that watch over the Islanders. Each of Jeju's villages has its own resident *Bonhyangdangshin*/본향당신^{original village shrine god}. As their name makes clear, they are the deified founding ancestors of the village.[80] Their shrines are like village halls where locals, particularly women, report all the important events of their lives: the births of children, deaths of relatives, the state of the year's harvest and even trips to the mainland.[81]

As for the ancestors of the village gods themselves, the *Songdang Bonpuri*/송당본풀이 introduces '**Socheonguk/소천국**' and his wife Baekju-ddo/백주또. Together, they bore twenty-eight daughters and eighteen sons, each of whom founded a village and became its Bonhyangdangshin.

Though it was certainly a fruitful marriage, it was not a happy one. For one, Socheonguk and Baekju-ddo came from different worlds. While he was a hunter native to Jeju, she was an agriculturalist from China. Old habits die hard, and Socheonguk's attempt to enter her world and start farming ended in disaster.

One day, while he was busy ploughing the fields, a passing monk ate his lunch. This was quite a feat, for Socheonguk had a voracious appetite, and Baekju-ddo had prepared him nine bowls of rice and nine bowls of broth. When Socheonguk found these eighteen bowls completely empty, he almost fainted. Exhausted from his work, he felt that if he didn't eat anything right away, he would surely starve.

The only thing that could save him from this hunger was the one thing he needed most. Though a source of invaluable labour, the cow he used to pull his plough was now no more to him than his next meal. He killed the poor creature and skinned it with fingernails like metal rakes. But even after cooking and eating the cow in its entirety, he was still hungry. Now, with no cow of his own, he killed and devoured a cow in the neighbouring field. Then and only then was he full at last.

Alas, the act of filling his cavernous stomach came

at a great cost. When Baekju-ddo found out what had happened, she was shocked beyond belief. Her own husband was a thief of the worst kind. He had deprived not only his own family but also his neighbour of years of labour. Thus, Baekju-ddo declared on the spot that their marriage was at an end. She refused to go on living with such a criminal.

Try as he might, Socheonguk was unable to change her mind. He gathered his things and was gone that very same day. Without his wife's civilising influence, he quickly reverted to his old, primitive ways. He set up his new home within a cave on the slopes of the volcano of Hallasan/한라산^{the volcano at the centre of Jeju} and returned to his life as a hunter, and a hunter he remains, now enshrined as the hunting god of the Alsondang Shrine/알손당.[82]

It is fitting that Socheonguk went to live on Hallasan. Blanketed in dense forest, it is the main hunting ground of the Island. But it is much more than just that. Visible from every part of the Island and dominating a vast portion of its interior, Hallasan has long been considered the home of gods. Its very name conveys its majesty, with Halla translating to 'The peak that drags down the Milky Way'.[83]

Because of its importance in the local hunting culture, and the belief in its divinity, many of the hunting gods were thought to have an intimate connection with

Hallasan. Hence, more often than not, they too were believed to be Mountain Gods, or as they're called in Korea, *Sanshin*/산신.

But not all of the Island's Sanshin reside on Hallasan itself. The Oreum[volcanic hill] of Gonaebong/고내봉 on the northwest coast is home to a **Sanshin Baekgwan/산신백관**[84]. *Baekgwan*/백관/百官[Hundred Ministers] was a historical term used in Korea to refer to various high ranking government officials. Consequently, the title also confers great prestige to the gods. It is only granted to Sanshin who are accomplished in some kind of field of study such as Pungsu-ji-ri/풍수지리[feng shui] or Cheonmun-ji-ri/천문지리[astronomical geography].[85]

고내봉의 산신백관
Sanshin Baekgwan of Gonaebong

In spite of his lofty title, this Sanshin was not the brightest of his kind. For one thing, he didn't understand how to attract worshippers. After enshrining himself atop Gonaebong, he hungrily awaited offerings. But though he waited and waited, none came. Confused, he called his human friend Chorip-dongee/초립동이 to help him understand why. Chorip-dongee was nonplussed. Of course, he had received no food, for he had just sat on the hill all this time. He told the Sanshin that if he wanted food, he would have to be more proactive. Chorip-dongee advised him to fire arrows in all four directions so that they landed at each of the entrances of the nearby village. When the arrows landed, disease would spread and life would become so uncomfortable that the residents would be forced to placate the god with food.

The Sanshin did as Chorip-dongee said, and soon, the disease had spread throughout the whole village. This time, the villagers sought not the advice of their shaman but instead that of their local goddess, *Songshee Halmang*/송씨 할망[grandmother Song]. She told them about Sanshin Baekgwan and advised them to make offerings to him and build a shrine for him on the purest, sunniest part of Gonaebong.

The villagers did as they were told, and sure enough, the disease that had afflicted them soon subsided. The shrine was in such a good spot moreover that soon other gods began to flock to it. In total, the Sanshin ended up sharing his shrine with four others, his loyal friend Chorip-dongee included.[86]

Not all of the island's guardians have the luxury of their own shrine or a complex origin story. One such guardian is the **Bangsatap/방사탑**. Much simpler in design yet much more visible than Jeju's shrines, it takes the form of a large, circular mound of stones.

To understand its purpose, we need only look at its name. The Hanja character Bang/방/防, means 'to block' or 'to interrupt'; the character Sa/사/邪, means 'evil'; and the Tap/탑/塔, means 'tower' or more specifically 'pagoda'. Therefore, the name as a whole directly translates to 'Evil blocking tower', although the translation used on information boards in Jeju, 'Evil expelling tower', has a better ring to it.[87]

Though 'Bangsatap' is the most widely accepted term, it is far from the only name given to these towers. Almost every village has a different name with which they refer to their own Bangsatap. These include: Dap/탑, Dapdani/탑단이, Geo-uk/거욱, Geowak/거왁, and Geo-okdae/거옥대.[88]

방사탑
Bangsatap

The placement of these towers is largely dictated by the principles of Pungsujiri/풍수지리. A key concern in Pungsujiri is to find shelter from life-destroying winds. In particular, the flow of wind towards one's house must at least be partially hindered. This lethal wind, the Haepung/해풍[harmful wind], can be blocked by the construction of walls or the planting of trees around one's home.[89] In terms of sheltering an entire village, though, both methods are either too costly or too time-consuming. The construction of a Bangsatap is far more economical. While it does not require great expense, its placement requires careful consideration. It must stand in the most exposed direction of the village.

A prime example of a dangerously exposed village is the walled settlement of Daejeongseong/대정성 in Inseong-li/인성리 in southwest Jeju. To its south stretches the plain of Albengdi/알뱅디, said from long ago to be the source of fires that ravage the area's farms. These fires only came to an end after the construction of four Bangsatap towers, three of which remain today.

But these three towers are not mere mounds of stones. Like many others, they are assisted in their defence of the village by the stone figures which stand atop them: either a rock resembling a bird or a small Dolhareubang/돌하르방.

돌하르방
Dolhareubang

Of all the gods of Jeju, none have been so warmly embraced by Koreans as '**Dolhareubang/돌하르방**' ^stone grandfather^. With his bulging pupilless eyes, broad nose, mushroom hat, and often a faint smile on his lips, he cuts a friendly figure. Though often rather comical due to his oversized features, he has a certain dignity about him, a certain air of strength; always standing upright with two powerful hands clutching his chest. As his name suggests, he is made from stone, but not just any stone. His body is made up of the same stone which makes up the body of the Island: Hyeonmu-am/현무암, Jeju's distinctive pockmarked basalt.

Before he became an ambassador for tourism, he was a *Suhoshin* ^a guardian deity^ like Bangsatap Towers. Moreover, like the Bangsatap Towers of Albengdi, Dolhareubang also sometimes appear in groups of four. In the villages of Daejeong Hyeonseong/대정현성 and Seongeub-li/성읍리, which have maintained their formidable stone walls of old, groups of four Dolhareubang statues stand guard in front of their gates. Two pairs of Dolhareubang stand facing each other, watchful for any unwanted intruders.

However, the Dolhareubang do more than just stand guard. They also wield great powers of fertility. To find out why, we need to return to their appearance. The mushroom-like hat worn by the Dolhareubang is possibly an imitation of Beonggeoji/벙거지^{the traditional bucket hat} worn by many men in the Joseon Dynasty era. This hat was said to resemble a phallus when seen from either the back or the sides, and therefore became a symbol of masculine, Yang energy/양기.

Another part of the Dolhareubang's appearance which hints at its powers of fertility is its nose. In Korea, a bulging nose like that of the Dolhareubang was seen as a sign of virility. Hence the phrase '*Jangmo-neun Jotgetnei Jangin Ko-ga Keoseo*/장모는 좋겠네 장인 코가 커서', meaning 'It's good for the mother-in-law that the father-in-law has a big nose'.[90]

For this reason, the Dolhareubang's nose became a prime target for those who wanted to conceive. To absorb its powers of fertility, the women of Jeju secretly scraped off pieces in the dead of night and mixed them with water to drink.[91]

Though he has come to mean so much to the people of Jeju, Dolhareubang has not been on the Island for long. The earliest written record of Dolhareubang, or Ongjungseok/옹중석 as they were called originally, is 1754.[92] It is most likely then, that they are not native in origin. Several theories connect Dolhareubang to statues all across Northeast Asia. These include:

- The Jangseung/장승 statues of mainland Korea.
- The Chinese statues of the Chin Dynasty General Ruan Wengzhong/阮翁仲 or Wan Ongjung/완옹중 as he is known in Korean.[93]
- The Harabarakan statues of Mongolia.[94]

Chapter Eight. Jeju Protecting & Attacking Cards

Kim Tongjeong
Gwangyangdangshin
Coral Hacnyeo
Jang Gilson

김통정
Kim Tongjeong

Not every foreign visitor deserved as warm a welcome as Dolhareubang. While he brought protection and fertility to the Islanders, other foreigners brought only death and destruction. One such foreigner was **Kim Tongjeong/김통정**, a Goryeo Dynasty(918-1392) General of the Sambyeolcho/삼별초[three elite patrols].

The Sambyeolcho army rose up in rebellion in 1270 after the King of Goryeo surrendered to the Mongols. They were disgusted by the idea of vassalage to a people they considered barbarians. Basing themselves on the Island of Jindo/진도 to the southwest, the Sambyeolcho's generals launched raids across the Peninsula. Soon, though, they faced a combined force of not only Goryeo but also Mongol forces, and in 1271 were forced off the Island.

One of the Sambyeolcho generals, Bae Jungson/배중손 was killed in the invasion, but another general, Kim Tongjeong/김통정 survived and managed to escape with the remaining troops. He fled to Jeju and prepared for a final stand. Against such overwhelming enemy forces, he could do nothing else. When the joint Mongol-Goryeo forces invaded the Island in 1273, the Sambyeolcho army was annihilated and Kim Tongjeong was killed. That being said, the memory of their resistance lived on, and General Kim Tongjeong became a figure of legend.[95]

Though on the mainland he is considered a martyr, in many of the legends of Jeju, he is cast instead as a villain. In one such story, Kim began to oppress the locals as soon as he arrived on the Island, conscripting them as labourers to prepare his defences. They slaved away to construct great earthen walls, which still stand today in the district of Aewol-eup/애월읍, but even after the walls were finished, they received no respite. Kim had his soldiers seize much of their precious crops and then lock them up within his newly made fortress. Meanwhile, the crops that he spared were left to rot in the fields as the locals were too exhausted to reap them.[96]

But even after all this suffering he had caused, Kim Tongjeong was not yet satisfied with his defences. As a final precaution, he had ashes scattered along the tops of the walls and swept into the air by soldiers wielding horsehair brooms. Now, his fortress seemed truly impregnable. Ash streamed out and blanketed the whole Island so it was impossible to distinguish between the earth and the sky. Any human enemies would surely get lost in the smog.

However, unfortunately for him, this last act had made him enemies of a different sort: they were **Gwangyangdangshin/광양당신** and his two younger brothers. According to the *Gwangyangdang Bonpuri*/광양당 본풀이,[97] they were the divine sons of Socheonguk and Baekju-ddo. Gwangyangdangshin was the most powerful of the three brothers, known as the protector god of Hallasan.

As soon as darkness began to cover the world, the three brother gods sprang into action. Though an outsider, Kim knew there was something off about the three men. When he saw them approaching, he realised his defences would be of little use and made his escape. He was no ordinary man either and used magic to speed away on a Muswe Bangseok/무쇠방석 ^{an iron sitting cushion}. This, however, was no sure ticket to safety. As he floated

광양당신
Gwangyangdangshin

over the sea, he fell afoul of a different enemy. The dragon kings of the four seas caught sight of him and started dragging the sitting cushion down into the waters. Soon, he was forced to abandon it, narrowly avoiding the clutches of the dragons below. He transformed into a hawk and continued his flight.

Little did he know that the three brothers also possessed powers of flight and transformation. They were hot in pursuit behind him, now in the form of two birds and a mosquito. When they had almost caught up, Kim grew curious about the noises coming from behind him: a thunderous flapping of feathered wings and the high-pitched whining of tiny chitinous wings. Still clad in armour of metal scales, he was almost impervious to attack, but when he turned his neck to look back, he exposed his single weak spot. This was the moment his enemies had been waiting for. As soon as Kim turned his neck, Gwangyangdangshin, now in hawk form, plunged a dagger into the chink in his armour. Kim died at once, his blood scattering over the waves below.[98]

Kim was not the only invader who was given a watery grave by Gwangyangdangshin. Another of his victims was Gojongdalee(Hojongdan)/고종달이(호종단), a Chinese geomancer. According to legend, he was dispatched by none other than Qin Shi Huang himself to travel to Jeju and use his knowledge of Pungsujiri (Feng

Shui) to cripple the power of the Island. As we have seen already, Pungsujiri is the belief that a vital energy flows beneath the earth and influences humans' fortunes. Gojongdalee was tasked with severing these flows so they would not reach the places where the Islanders lived. Through doing so, he hoped to ensure that no heroes would ever be born on the Island who could challenge the authority of the Chinese emperor.

At first, he was very successful. He blocked up springs all across Jeju and even managed to track down and maim a dragon. This dragon lived within the cliff of Yongmeori/용머리^{dragon head}, in the southwest of Jeju, at the foot of Sanbangsan/산방산^{Sanbang Mountain}. At that time, it was alive and well, receiving a flow of vital energy from the peak of Hallasan and in turn passing this energy on to the surrounding area. Yet though his own emperor bore the emblem of a dragon upon his breast, Gojongdalee had no mercy for the poor creature. He began by slicing off its tail and then cut its back into two pieces. As he did so, a torrent of blood gushed out into the surrounding ocean, and an agonised howl echoed beneath Sanbangsan.

This act had a devastating impact on both the land and its people. From then on, the people of Jeju were made leaderless as no great kings could be born on the Island. Furthermore, the landscape of Jeju was forever scarred, with the signs of the dragon's mutilation still visible in the strange patterns of the Yongmeori cliffs.

By this point, Jeju had been badly crippled, but Gojongdalee was not finished. He still had one last stop before he sailed back home: the Chagwido/차귀도 ^{Chagwi Island} just off the west coast of Jeju. Unfortunately for him, that was where Jeju finally fought back. As he sailed towards the Island, ready to sever another flow of energy, he noticed a hawk flying towards him. At first, he didn't pay it much attention, but as it got closer, he noticed how it stirred up the waters below. A tidal wave was surging in its shadow, a wave from which there was no escape. As the hawk passed overhead, the wave crashed into the ship and dealt it a fatal blow. The vessel splintered into matchwood, and its crew were thrown into the seething ocean. The entire crew, Go jongdalee included, had no chance of survival, and every one of them was drowned.

Meanwhile, the hawk circling above looked down in satisfaction. It was none other than Gwangyangdangshin/광양당신, victorious once again over the enemies of Jeju.

One enemy Gwangyangdangshin did not vanquish was the dreaded Mamashin/마마신 ^{the god of smallpox}. Smallpox was particularly virulent during the Joseon Dynasty era and the Koreans' fear of this deity is apparent in her name. Mama/마마 was the highest title a woman could receive in Korea, thereby demonstrating the god's unquestionable authority.[99]

In the distant past, Mamashin was said to visit Jeju once every year. She was never welcome, but at least the Islanders could plan for her arrival, which was always sometime between spring and autumn. Each year, the Islanders greeted her with a sumptuous feast, and each year, she left the Island content, having spared its people the worst of her powers. This was until one year, when she complained that the food they had prepared for her was not enough.

She immediately started spreading smallpox to every part of the Island. Wherever the Islanders sought refuge, the disease found them. They tried blocking it with great stone walls and they tried hiding in caves, but all their efforts were in vain.

Nevertheless, all hope was not lost. The Islanders knew of a way to banish Mamashin. Within Donghae Yonggung/동해용궁^{east sea dragon palace}, grew a special kind of coral which could expel smallpox. Unfortunately, retrieving the coral was fraught with dangers, and everyone was too nervous to volunteer. Everyone that is except one young girl from

산호 해녀
Coral Haenyeo

the southern port of Moseulpo/모슬포^{sandy harbour}, a girl who had just begun work as a Jamsu/잠수^{diver}.

Jamsu is the original title for the Island's diver women, *Haenyeo*/해녀. Jamsu, as we shall call the girl since she is given no name in the story, was an *Aegi-jamsu*/애기잠수^{baby diver}.[100] As this title suggests, she had little experience. In fact, she had only just learnt to swim.

What she lacked in experience, she more than made up for in determination. Plunging into the cold ocean, she swam all the way to the East Sea Dragon Palace. Yet more intractable than the fathomless sea was the East Sea Dragon King himself. No matter how much Jamsu begged, he refused to relinquish the sacred coral. It was, he told her, a priceless treasure belonging only to the palace, and as such, he would never let it leave the premises. Fortunately, though, he wasn't completely indifferent to the fate of the Islanders. In place of the coral, he would dispatch a mighty army to defeat Mamashin in battle.

On the way back to the surface, this army was joined by a legion of Bawi-Shinryeong/바위신령^{rock spirits}. Together, they were a formidable force, and when they reached the surface, the Islanders rejoiced, believing their salvation had come at last. Alas, they were sadly mistaken. Even such an army could not withstand the onslaught of Mamashin and her allies. Soon, their bodies lay strewn across the land. The cold bodies of the rock spirits can be found even now, still pockmarked with holes made by the spears and arrows of Mamashin's soldiers.

Then, as if things could not get any worse, the Islanders were dismayed to find yet another casualty of war. As the high tide rolled in, the body of courageous little Jamsu washed up on the shore. But when the Islanders approached her body, a miraculous transformation took place. A mist of many colours descended upon her, and when it cleared, Jamsu was gone, but in her place was a radiant sprig of coral, the coral of the East Sea Dragon Palace. Jamsu had sacrificed herself for the good of the Island, and so its people were able at last to drive Mamashin from its shores.[101]

Another unlikely hero in Jeju mythology is the giant '**Jang Gilson/장길손**'. A recurring character in Korea's oral tradition, there are several variants of Jang Gilson's exploits as well as parallel stories of similar giants. Yet in all his legends, Jang Gilson is depicted as belonging to one of the more benign species of giant. He is at his core a comical and rather pitiful figure.

Long ago, he was said to roam the earth, covering rivers and forests in a single stride. But Jang Gilson was not proud of his great size. He was, in fact, a victim of his great stature. No meal could fill his cavernous stom-

장길손
Jang Gilson

ach, and no garment could cover his immeasurable bulk. So it was that he wandered the world in abject misery, forever hungry and forever exposed to the elements. Only his private parts were protected, covered by a crude skirt of leaves.

But one day, Jang Gilson found himself in the south of Korea and there, at last, his fortunes began to change. The locals did not scatter and hide when they saw him coming. They welcomed him as an honoured guest, lavishing him with a feast fit for a king. The impossible came true as Jang Gilson was at last able to eat his fill. This, moreover, was not the limit of the people's compassion. They set about creating an enormous set of clothes, big enough even for one such as him. When it was finished and Jang Gilson was clothed, he was beside himself with joy.

In a cruel twist of fate, his show of appreciation for their gifts caused the Koreans to turn against him. He was so happy with his new clothing that he sprang to his feet and began dancing a jig. Unfortunately, the shadow cast by his dancing form blocked out the sun, and so, all the crops began to wither and die. For this reason, he was banished from the land. Forced back northwards, his ravenous hunger soon returned, but this time, there was no one to feed him. In desperation, he resorted to eating dirt and rocks, but this, of course, did not sit well with his stomach. What followed was a rapid evacuation from both ends. Moreover, the volume of what came out was so great that it changed the landscape of the entire region.

His vomit hardened into the volcano of Baekdusan/백두산[Baekdu Mountain], the highest peak on the entire Korean Peninsula, his tears turned into two great rivers, and the violent torrent of his urine severed a land bridge between Korea and Japan. His diarrhoea was so explosive that pieces flew in all directions. One oval piece landed in the seas to the south of Korea, and that, at least according to this story, became the Isle of Jeju.[102]

Chapter Nine. Fertility God Cards

Samseung Halmang
Gu-Samseung Halmang
Shinsomi

삼승할망
Samseung Halmang

A more famous and far more majestic figure credited with the creation of Jeju is Seolmundae Halmang/설문대할망. Unlike Jang Gilson, she was driven by a vision, not by an upset stomach. She made Jeju to be a paradise, a small but harmonious land with flat edges and a great mountain at its centre. In one story, she even gave her own life to make the Island the best it could be. She became one with her creation, plunging into the bottomless lake atop Muljangol Oreum/물장올 오름. From then on, all of the streams that flow down the ninety-nine valleys of Hallasan were imbued with her essence. Her sons, the Five Hundred Generals/오백장군 were stricken with grief; they wandered the slopes of Hallasan, searching in vain for their lost mother. Such was their grief that they were turned to stone, but from their sorrow sprung new life. Azaleas thrived in the soil saturated by their tears and even now, every spring the mountain is dyed red by their blossoms.[103]

She loves the Islanders as a grandmother loves her grandchildren, hence the title *Halmang*/할망, the word for 'grandmother' in Jeju dialect, though it also refers to any goddess regardless of her age.

Another Halmang with equally boundless love for the Islanders is '**Samseung Halmang/삼승할망**[grandmother of the world of the conception]',[104] As her name suggests, she is a goddess of fertility, the Island's equivalent to 'Samshin Halmeoni/삼신할머니', the goddess of fertility on the mainland.

She favours the Islanders with the miracles of birth and conception. But against her enemies, she wields these as weapons. The *Manura Bonpuri*/마누라 본풀이[wife Bonpuri] tells the story of how she used these powers to humble mighty Daebyeolsang/대별상[the male incarnation of Mamashin]. After he afflicted the Island's children with smallpox, she worked her magic to impregnate Daebyeolsang's wife, Seoshinguk Manura/서신국 마누라, but then refused to deliver the baby.

Months after her due date, Seoshinguk Manura was no closer to giving birth. Though her body was swollen like a vase, the baby would not come out. The strain was too much to bear, and death seemed imminent for both mother and child. In the end, Daebyeolsang had to swallow his pride and beg Samseung Halmang for forgiveness. However, Samseung Halmang wanted much more than just an apology. In penance, Daebyeolsang shaved his head and dressed as a monk. Most humiliating of all were the restrictions placed on his powers. He was forced to promise that from then on, he would only ever infect children with chickenpox.

Unfortunately, though, Daebyeolsang is far from the only threat to the Island's children. Samseung Halmang also protects them from her disgruntled predecessor, **Gu-Samseung Halmang/구삼승할망** the old Samseung grandmother.

Regardless of what she became, this goddess is much more sympathetic than Daebyeolsang. After all, she was set up to fail. She was cast out of her home, the East Sea Dragon Palace, at a young age, and she was only ever educated on how to ensure the conception of children but knew nothing of their delivery. That was why Cheonjiwang/천지왕 king of heaven and earth, the supreme god of the Jeju pantheon, had her replaced with another young woman. She tried to appeal his decision, and in response he declared a competition between the two. To prove they were the true Samseung Halmang, all the two contenders had to do was plant a flower. They were each given a single seed but this they were forced to plant in the most barren of soils: a bed of sand.

Nevertheless, with the love and care of the Samseung Halmang, life can take root in the most unlikely of places. Against all odds, flowers soon sprouted from both plots of land. But while the new Samseung Halmang grew a beautiful bouquet of radiant blossoms, all that her predecessor managed to grow was the miserable *Myeolmang-ggot*/멸망꽃 the flower of destruction.

No one who saw those two flowers was in any doubt about who won the challenge. Thus, with no further ado, Cheonjiwang declared his decision final.

구삼승할망
Gu-Samseung Halmang

Gu-samseung Halmang, as she was then known, would be responsible not for the well-being of living babies but for the souls of those who died. To this end, she would be forced to descend to Jeoseung/저승 the 'Otherworld', the land of the dead.

This consolation prize was cold comfort for Gu-Samseung Halmang. Determined to get revenge, she tore a sprig off one of the flowers grown by her competitor. This, she told the horrified onlookers, would ensure that every baby would be wracked by disease. Only for the first hundred days after their birth would they be spared.

Even Cheonjiwang was powerless to undo this curse. It was fortunate indeed then that he had found the perfect woman for the new Samseung Halmang. She offered her predecessor a compromise, assuring her that she would not be forgotten in the gloom of Jeoseung. In return for the retraction of her curse, she would receive offerings from all parents when their baby reached the one-hundred-day mark.

This, Gu-Samseung Halmang realised, was the best offer she would get. She could not deny the superior ability of the new Samseung Halmang and, at the very least it did give her a role in life, a role moreover that she could actually fulfil. Therefore, she accepted the deal and prostrated before Cheonjiwang. With the flower of destruction in one hand, she set off for Jeoseung and with that she was gone from the world of the living.[105]

신소미
Shinsomi

The new Samseung Halmang then set about establishing her position in the living world. She raised a grand pavilion in which to live, and she resides there even now, surrounded by countless helpers. Among these are the **Shinsomi/신소미**, young maidens who look after the flowers of the Seocheonggotbat/서천꽃밭^{the western heaven flower fields}. They are the spirits of girls who died before the age of fifteen.

As compensation for their untimely deaths they have been given the role of looking after the lives of others. Each of the flowers they care for represents the life of a human in the world of men below.[106] Unfortunately, though, the shinsomi are not free from the divisions of the living world even in the next life. They water the flowers using the dishes they ate from as children. This means that while the wealthier children use dishes made from silver or bronze, the poor children are forced to use only crude dishes made from gourds.[107]

Chapter Ten. Farming God Cards

~~~~~~~~~~~~~~~~~~~~~~~~

Jacheongbi
Jeongsoonamee Owl
King Seosoo's Daughter

자청비
Jacheongbi

Another goddess with intimate knowledge of the Seocheonggotbat/서천꽃밭^{the western heaven flower fields} is **Jacheongbi/자청비**. She is arguably the most multi-talented and multifaceted of all Jeju's goddesses. In the story of her origin, the *Segyeong Bonpuri*/세경본풀이^{farmland Bonpuri}, she plays the role of a gifted student, hunter, seamstress, monk, general, devoted wife and even devoted husband. But most important of all is her role as a farming goddess. This is apparent in her name, as 'Jacheongbi' means the 'rain that falls of its own accord'. As the goddess of agriculture, she is intimately connected with the rain that fertilises the ground and yields an abundant harvest. Another interpretation of her name is that if you take it upon yourself to work for the harvest (i.e. pray and make offerings to Jacheongbi), the rain will fall, and your wish will be granted.

She is also known as Jungsegyeong-shin/중세경신 ^(the middle farmland god) who brought the 'Five Grains'[108] down from the heavens to the world of men below. Much of the Segyeong Bonpuri concerns her efforts to reunite with her lost love, Mundoryeong^(bachelor Mun). He was a man of heaven and the son of the Jade Emperor/옥황상제. Upon his marriage to Jacheongbi, he became Sangsegyeong-shin/상세경신^(the high farmland god). Due to the place of his birth, Mundoryeong is given the role of bringing the all-important rains from heaven.

Their love story was one of great adversity, and it was not without its casualties. One of these was **Jeongsoonamee/정수남이**, a cattle herder working for Jacheongbi's family. Though he was several social classes her inferior, he was completely enamoured with his young mistress. He was not bothered by her love for Mundoryeong. In fact, he used this to take advantage of her. Sometime after Mundoryeong had been called back to the heavens, Jeongsoonamee told Jacheongbi that he had seen him back down on earth frolicking with heavenly maidens in a pool on the slopes of Hallasan.

This was a lie, a ploy to lure his mistress somewhere where she wouldn't be able to resist his advances.

Though Jacheongbi was certainly intelligent, her mind was clouded with the thought of seeing her beloved once again. She believed the lie, commanding Jeongsoonamee to ready two horses and lead her to the pool at once. By the time she realised what was really going on, they were alone in a secluded valley, and the sun was about to set.

However, Jacheongbi was no damsel in distress. Jeongsoonamee had planned this ambush well, but Jacheongbi would outfox him yet. She feigned attraction, thanking Jeongsoonamee for bringing her to such a well-hidden getaway. Yet before he could embrace her, she asked him if he really wanted her to freeze in the chill night air.

Surely they were not about to consummate their love out in the open like beasts? That was how she

정수남이 부엉이
Jeongsoonamee Owl

tricked him into making an *Oom-mak*/움막^{a small dugout shelter}. But every time he finished one of its walls, Jacheongbi poked holes in it so he would have to build it once again. This continued for much of the night until Jeongsoonamee was so exhausted that he fell asleep. That was when he became the victim. Jacheongbi broke off a thorny vine from a nearby bush and ran it through Jeongsoonamee's ear until it came out from the other side.

To Jacheongbi, this was a justifiable murder. Her parents, however, did not agree. When they heard of what she had done, they were horrified and kicked her out of their home. That was how Jacheongbi made her first trip to the Seocheonggotbat. In an effort to seek their forgiveness, Jacheongbi sought the flowers of resurrection with which to revive Jeongsoonamee.

But when she finally entered the fields, she was surprised to find him alive and well. Still, he wasn't the same Jeongsoonamee she had known before. He had lost his human body. His resentful spirit had been reborn instead in the body of an owl. This was a fitting fate for a man unable to control his animal urges. It meant that both his body and name described his true self. His bestial nature is encapsulated in his extended name, Jeong-ee-eu-shin Jeongsoonamee/정이으신정수남이, with Jeong-ee-eu-shin the word in Jeju dialect for *jeong-ee eopda*/정이 없다^{lacking affection}.

Fitting though it may have been, his new incarnation was a disaster for the Seocheonggotbat and its caretakers. Every time he hooted, the flowers of the fields shrivelled and died.

Jacheongbi had come at the right time then. Owl or no owl, she was hell-bent on tracking him down, and she knew exactly how to catch him. Wandering into the sea of flowers, Jacheongbi enticed him by taking off all her clothes and lying down on top of them. Then, when the lustful owl swooped down from above, she shot it down with a bow and arrow.

This second murder was soon followed by a resurrection. Picking four kinds of flowers from the fields, she went all the way back to the valley where now only Jeongsoonamee's skeleton remained. She scattered the flowers over his bones, and after hitting his body three times with a bamboo cane, he awoke, a man once more. However, he would not remain a man. He eventually became a god of agriculture, Hasegyeong-shin/하세경신 ^{the low farmland god}. A cowherd in life, he is now believed to protect all cattle and give them the strength they need to pull the ploughs that cultivate the earth.

Meanwhile, Jacheongbi's beloved Mundoryeong had an unwanted admirer of his own, Seosoo-wang Ddanimagi/서수왕 따님아기^{King Seosoo's Daughter}. He was originally betrothed to her, not Jacheongbi. When he broke off the engagement, she was devastated. In a fit of rage, she burnt the wedding invitations he had returned to her and drank their ashes with water. That would be her last contact with the outside world. She retreated to her bedroom and locked the door behind her. The door remained closed for a hundred days, and when her family finally forced it open, they found her long dead. There was no corpse. Such was her resentment that the instant she died, she transformed into a flock of four malicious birds. These plague humanity even now, sowing strife between husband and wife. They also cause us physical pain:

◆ From her head emerged
the Dutong-sae/두통새[headache bird].

◆ From her eyes emerged
the Heulgit-sae/흘깃새[glower bird].

◆ From her nose emerged
the Aksum-sae/악숨새[troubled breathing bird].

◆ From her mouth emerged
the Bubugan-Iganjil-sae/
부부간 이간질새[trouble between husband and wife bird].

In the same way that we must endure the presence of Noiljedaegwi-il's Daughter within our home, we must also provide for the troubled soul of Seosoo-Wang Ddanimagi/서수왕 따님아기^{King Seosoo's Daughter} at our wedding. To avoid her curse, newly-weds set aside food for her soul at their wedding feast.[109]

It is striking then that both the resentful souls of Jeongsoonamee and Seosoo-Wang Ddanimagi transform into birds. The question is, why? Of course, cultures the world over have visualised the soul as a bird, fluttering away from its body upon death. In Jeju, however, the answer also lies in language. The Korean word for bird is Sae/새, and the Hanja character for evil or malice is Sa/사/邪, but in Jeju dialect, this can also be pronounced as Sae. Thus the word Sae has come to embody both meanings, and birds have become regarded as manifestations of evil energy.[110]

서수왕 따님아기
King Seosoo's Daughter

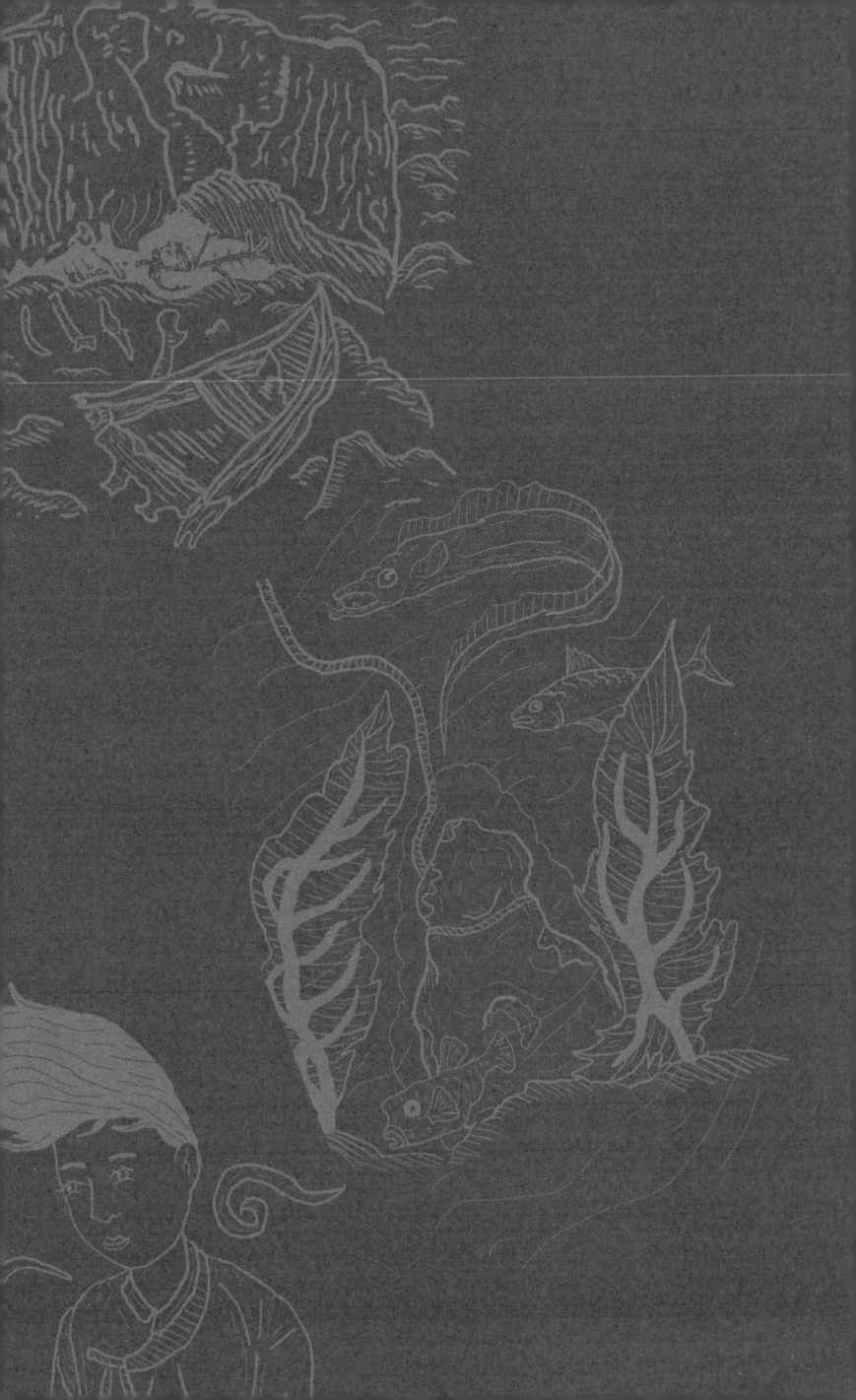

Chapter Eleven.
Sea God Cards

~~~~~~~~~~

Yeongdeung Halmang
Waenoonbegi
Hol-eomongdol
Aegi-oepgae
Mireukdol

영등할망
Yeongdeung Halmang

Living on Samjaedo/삼재도^{the island of three disasters}, the farmers of Jeju have often struggled to make ends meet. So it is no wonder they have sought protection from gods, such as Jacheongbi and Baekju-ddo.

Arguably, though, no force in nature is as fickle and unpredictable as the sea. Accordingly, it is the Island's fishermen and diver women, the Haenyeo/해녀, who rely most heavily on the shamanist gods of old.

One such god is Yeongdeungshin/영등신, the god of wind. As an embodiment of one of the Island's 'Three Abundances', Yeongdeungshin has many incarnations: civil servants, kings, men and women. On Jeju, the most famous of these is Yeongdeung Halmang/영등할망^{Yeoungde-}

ung grandmother. In one variant of the *Yeongdeung Bonpuri*/영등본풀이 recorded by Kim Sunee(김순이), she takes the form of a beautiful young woman living in a distant sea.

There, Yeongdeung Halmang was alone until one fateful day when a ship appeared on the horizon. A typhoon had blown it off course, and now it was barely keeping afloat. Its mast was broken, and its sails were torn to shreds. Thus, there was nothing its crew could do to stop it from drifting towards the rocky cliffs of the unknown land that lay ahead.

That land was the home of the **Waenoonbegi/외눈배기**^{one-eyed ones}, a race of man-eating, one-eyed giants. However, luck was on the sailors' side, as they were first spotted not by any of the Waenoonbegi but by Yeongdeung. She blew them under the shadows of the great rock of Wangbawi/왕바위^{king rock}, from which she hung her seaweed skirt so that they were hidden from hungry eyes. Shortly afterwards, the Waenoonbegi arrived, asking her if she had seen the fishing boat, which they described as full of tasty Banchan/반찬^{side dishes}. Yeongdeung feigned ignorance, saying she had seen no sign of such a thing and was merely drying her hair on the powerful winds that struck the rock.

As the last of the Waenoonbegi lumbered off, the sailors thanked her profusely. Several days later, the men had fixed up the ship and were ready to sail back home.

외눈배기
Waenoonbegi

However, Yeongdeung told them they needed more than a seaworthy vessel in order to return. From the shores of this cursed isle to the shores of their home, they must chant the name 'Ganam Bosal, Ganam Bosal/가남보살 _{Avalokitesvara, the bodhisattva of compassion}'. With that, The sailors were off, chanting as they caught a southerly wind. Alas, when they finally caught sight of their beloved home Jeju, they cried out in excitement. Having forgotten Yeongdeung's advice, they were then blown all the way back to the land of the giants.

Fortunately, Yeongdeung was once again the first to see them. Chiding them for their failure to do as they were told, she hid them again and sent them back home when the winds were right. This time, they focussed entirely on chanting the name of Ganam Bosal and did not even look up at the peak of Hallasan until their ship was deep within the harbour.

Their benefactor, Yeongdeung was not so lucky. She was caught by the Waenoonbegi. They were so angry that she had robbed them of 'tasty Banchan' that they killed her on the spot and then cut her body into three pieces. These they tossed unceremoniously into the sea. But like the Cheongu-agoo-daemeng-ee, it would take more than being dismembered to finish her off. Eventually, all three pieces floated to the isle of Jeju. Her head washed ashore on the isle of Udo/우도 cow island to the northeast, her body in nearby Seongsan/성산 and her legs in Hansu-li/한수리 on the northwest coast. When the sailors she had saved from the Waenoonbegi beheld this terrible sight, they were devastated. They knew, of course, that they had been the cause of her death. They called a shaman at once who held a 'Great Gut/큰굿' to pacify the spirit of Yeongdeung.

That night, a mysterious fog rose up from the waves. The whole island was surrounded by whirling winds. When the fog had cleared, Yeongdeung's body had been stitched back together.

Her body then floated like a flower petal upon the waves and a warm breeze, the breath of life began blowing across Jeju. From then on, once every year, Yeongdeung would be resurrected and return to Jeju for fifteen days, roaming around the northern coastline where the parts of her body had washed up. Her presence is the herald of spring. Her warmth thaws the frozen winter, and the life-bringing breath of spring flows over the isle, carrying seeds from the seas.[111]

While the northern coast may be under the protection of a Shin/신[god], the Yeoungdeungshin, the southern coast is plagued by several Gwi/귀[ghosts].

The first of these Gwi takes the form of a great volcanic boulder. Looming over the dried lava flow that makes up much of the shore of Shinsan-li/신산리 is the ominous form of '**Hol-eomongdol/흘어멍돌**[widow rock]'. A hardened lump of lava, it long ago decided to harden its heart against the locals. The area was plagued with accidents at sea, though strangely enough, the victims were always men. Suspicion was cast at the rock when people

흘어멍돌
Hol-eomongdol

realised that all the men who had died lived in houses from which it was visible.

But instead of trying to destroy '**Widow Rock**', the locals sought to neutralise it as a threat. To achieve this, they decided to humanise their igneous neighbour. Reasoning that the rock had killed men only because it was jealous of their wives, they decided to make it a partner of its own. On the top of a hill in the middle of the village, they erected a Namgeunseok/남근석[phallic rock]. No longer was it Hol-eomong/홀어멍[widow], and so, from then on, local legend tells us, the deaths stopped, and rock and man were able to live together in harmony.[112]

Such behaviour may appear odd, but it is not without precedent. Up until this very day, Korean geomancers warn of the dangers of places and objects with excess feminine energy. Feminine energy is, in other words, yin energy (eum-gi/음기), and it needs to be in balance with masculine yang energy (yang-gi/양기). With this in mind, a stone phallus is exactly the right tool to use when confronted with dangerously feminine surroundings.

Another example of dangerously feminine surroundings is Marado/마라도(end island), just off the southwest coast of Jeju. Inhabited by the soul of a resentful teenager, the mere sight of this island is said to be deadly. It is said to resemble a floating coffin and thereby projects negative energy at all those who see it. For this reason, in villages in the southwest of Jeju where Marado is visible, some tombs have an extra, high stone wall to block any view of the island.[113]

A five-minute walk away from the various seafood and black bean noodle restaurants the island is now famous for, in a much more secluded area lies a shrine to the spirit of a fourteen-year-old girl known only as '**Aegi-oepgae/애기업개**'. Here is her story:

Long ago, a girl named Heo-shee Aegi/허씨애기 [Ms. Heo] was abandoned by the side of the road. In order to survive, she had to take care of other children and carry them on her back. So it was that she came to be known instead as Aegi-oepgae/애기업개[baby carrier].

When she was fourteen, she decided to follow the Haenyeo[diver women] and sailed with them to the then-uninhabited Marado. But upon arrival, they found the waves too fierce to find any seafood and prepared to leave at once. Unfortunately, that too was rendered impossible by the stormy seas. Stranded on the island, their supplies soon ran out. But one day, Sanshin Daewang/산신대왕[great king mountain god] appeared in the dreams of one of the Haenyeo. He told her that they should leave a fourteen-year-old girl on the island, and then they would be allowed to sail back to the mainland.

The woman awoke and discussed the dream with

애기업개
Aegi-oepgae

the other Haenyeo. At first, it seemed too cruel to leave one of their own behind, but they knew that if they were stranded there for much longer, they would all starve to death. At last, they decided to concede to Sanshin Daewang's wish and quickly boarded their ship. To distract Aegi-oepgae, they told her to go fetch a Podaegi/포대기 _{a traditional quilt used for carrying a baby on one's back}, which they had left on the far side of the island. As soon as she was gone, the waves subsided, and the sea became calm. This was their chance. They cast off without a second thought, and Aegi-oepgae was left alone on the barren island.

When people returned to Marado the next year, they found that the poor girl had long since starved to death. Only her bones remained, picked clean by the crows. In order to placate her resentful spirit, they held an annual ritual in her memory and set up a Cheonye-odang/처녀당^{maiden shrine}, which later evolved into the Aegi-oepgae Halmangdang which stands there today.[114]

Fellow sea gods who know all too well the pain of being abandoned are the twin **Mireukdol/미륵돌**^{Maitreya stones} of Kimnyeong-li/김녕리 on Jeju's northwest coast. The Bonpuri to their shrine, the Kimnyeong Seomun Hareubangdang/김녕 서문하르방당^{the Kimnyeong west gate grandfather shrine} records how they were first found, and then abandoned by a local fisherman, Yunshee-Hareubang/윤씨하르방^{grandfather Mr. Yun}.

One day, when Yun went out to sea, he wasn't able to catch even a single fish. Instead, all that he managed to reel in was a strangely shaped rock. But as he pulled it up onto the boat, disappointment turned to wonder. As it emerged, the surrounding water bubbled and gleamed with a strange light that seemed to emanate from the rock itself.

From then on, Yun's fortunes began to change. The next few times he cast off, he caught whole sholes of Galchi/갈치^{cutlassfish}. Then, one day, not long after, Yun reeled in another strange rock. This gave him pause for thought. To find such a thing again could surely be no coincidence. Considering it an auspicious sign, he decided to set up a little shrine for the rocks on one side of his ship.

It proved to be a very wise decision. From then on, he caught not only cutlassfish but all manner of rarer, more expensive fish.

But sometime later, Yun reconsidered the value of the rocks. His boat wasn't all that large and he resented the rocks taking up the space that could otherwise be filled with fish. So, it was that he made a very unwise decision. He picked up the rocks and threw them back into the sea.

The very next day, a terrible storm struck the village. Its power was equalled by its duration: it continued for half a month, growing more powerful by the day. Soon, it was so strong that it not only prevented any ships from going fishing, but threatened to destroy the entire community. Roofs were blown off cottages, and the fields were flooded so that a famine seemed imminent.

Luckily, the abandoned Mireukdol were forgiving gods. One night, as the storm raged outside, Yun dreamt of a white-haired old man. He cut a pitiful figure, shivering from head to toe. He told Yun that he could not bear the cold any longer and begged him to house him somewhere warmer. For he was one of the Mireukdol, abandoned in the icy depths of the harbour. The sea, he told

Yun, was not their true home. They should be enshrined somewhere on land, and in return, they would grant all kinds of blessings to all kinds of people:

- ◆ To those who had no children, they would be Sanshin/산신^{birth gods/gods of fertility}:
This San/산 comes not from the Hanja character '山'^{mountain}, but rather '産'^{giving birth}.

- ◆ To those who desired peace and stability in their homes, they would be Sushin/수신^{protector gods}.

- ◆ To those wracked by poverty, they would be Jemulshin/재물신^{wealth gods}.

Finished with his plea, the white-haired old man left Yun and returned to the sea.

The next morning, Yun got up immediately and raced to the harbour. With no concern for the storm or the freezing waters, he dived into its depths to retrieve the Mireukdol. Much to his surprise, when he reached the sands of the seabed, he found both rocks standing side by side. Heavy though they were, he then carried them back to the surface, where he apologised for his thoughtless behaviour. Next, he took them to a sunny spot by the coast named Yeongdeungmul/영등물, where he enshrined them in an altar made of stone. There, the rocks remain. They have lived up to the promises they made to Yun. Even now, they are said to grant wealth, fertility and safe passage between Jeju and the mainland to all those who worship them.[115]

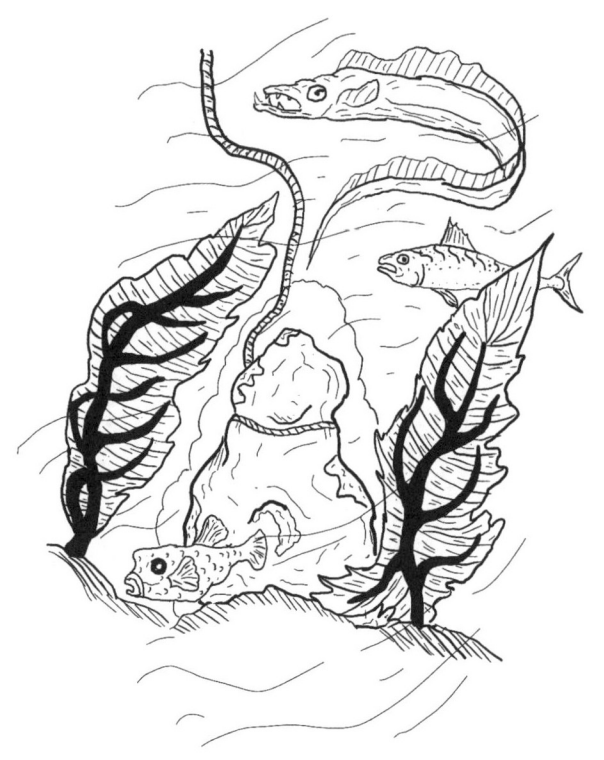

미륵돌
Mireukdol

Chapter Twelve. Dokkaebi Cards

Blood of a White Horse and Sorghum Rice
The Badger Rogue
Straw Ship

백마 피와 수수밥
Blood of a White Horse and Sorghum Rice

It is strange though that Mireukdol have become worshipped as sea gods on Jeju as their namesake, Mireuk/미륵, or Maitreya/मैत्रेय as he is known in the original Sanskrit, has no connection with the sea. Technically, he is not a god at all, he is the Buddha of the future, who will succeed the Shakyamuni Buddha of our age.[116]

Another group of unlikely sea god are the island's *Dokkaebi*/도깨비. Like the Mireukdol they were originally natives of the mainland and only took on their current role after they settled on Jeju's shores.

Without doubt, Dokkaebi are the most distinctive, most Korean of all the creatures of the Peninsula's mythology. Every Korean is familiar with the playful antics of Dokkaebi: their ability to shapeshift and conjure things into existence with the mere swing of their club. What many Koreans would not be familiar with is the notion of worshipping Dokkaebi. To those on the mainland, the Dokkaebi are generally little more than mischievous figures from folktales, but on Jeju they are revered as the bringers of manifold blessings: wealth, harvests, and plentiful fish. That being said, it is not always advisable to begin worshipping Dokkaebi. They are notoriously fickle and even when they are content, their mere presence can have a debilitating effect on nearby humans.

It is important then that their would-be worshipper be prepared, that he or she have the right tools and the right mindset. A good example of such a person is Song Yeonggam/송영감[elder song], the protagonist of the *Nakcheon-li Dokkaebi Shrine Bonpuri*/낙천리 도깨비당 본풀이.

As a Manchurian peasant, barely eking out an existence by picking medicinal herbs, he was initially enticed by the Dokkaebi's promise of wealth. When three Dokkaebi brothers asked for his worship, he immediately went out and caught a pig. This he offered up to his newfound patrons alongside Susu-bap/수수밥[sorghum rice] and Susu-ddeok/수수떡[sorghum rice cakes].

And so well fed were they, that they more than held up their end of the bargain. In no time at all, Song went from the poorest to the richest man in the village. Where once he languished in a hovel, now he lived it up in the tiled roof house of a nobleman. However, even the most spacious house seems cramped when you are sharing it with three Dokkaebi. In spite of all they had done for him, Song soon started to resent their company. It was common knowledge where his wealth had come from, and he hated the constant questions from those curious about his benefactors. Worse still, though he ate better than he had in his whole life, he was actually losing weight. As each day went by, he grew ever weaker. This, he suspected, was somehow the fault of the Dokkaebi.

Knowing that time was against him, he decided to take action before it was too late. He gathered the Dokkaebi one day and proposed the following wager: if they were able to pick all the crops in a nearby field in a single day, then he would worship them for the rest of his life; but if they failed, then the worship would end and they would have to leave.

Ever confident in their abilities, the Dokkaebi agreed at once. But this confidence was ill-founded. The field to which they were assigned was truly vast, and when the sun set, the work was still not complete. This was the turning point for Song in his relationship with the three brothers. They, who he had feared for so long, were now at his mercy and he was determined to seize this opportunity to rid himself of them for good. He tied the exhausted Dokkaebi to three trees and then cut each of them into four pieces. These he scattered far away from his home. Then, to stop their spirits returning for revenge, he had a **white horse slaughtered and scattered its blood all around his house.** This last act had made his house as secure as a fortress.

Each of the twelve animals of the Chinese zodiac are believed to correspond with one of the five elements, and the horse corresponds with fire. Therefore, like the element it embodies, the horse is believed to exude masculine yang energy.[117] This is the perfect antidote to the suffering caused by creatures which exude feminine yin energy such as ghosts and Dokkaebi. The colour white meanwhile has long been considered sacred by the people of Korea. The Hanja character for white, 'Baek/백' as it is pronounced in Korean, is 白. This is just one stroke away from the character for 日, meaning the sun or day: 日 pronounced as 'Il/일'. Accordingly, the colour white was associated with brightness. All manner of white animals were believed to be auspicious but when Koreans of old swore oaths to heaven, it was a white horse that they sacrificed.[118] The head of a white horse is thus doubly imbued with yang energy, embodying the yang energy of both fire and Heaven.

Meanwhile, one need not feel too sorry for the dismembered Dokkaebi: Each of the twelve pieces formed into a new Dokkaebi. Three of these later made their way to Jeju where they were enshrined as ancestor gods in the village of Nakcheon-li/낙천리. One was worshipped as Baetseonwang/뱃선왕 [king of ships], another as Sanshin Il-wol-ddo/산신일월또 [mountain god ancestor], and the last as Sotbul-mi/솥불미 [god of cauldrons and bellows].[119]

Another Dokkaebi who made his way to Jeju was **Osori Jamnom/오소리 잡놈** [The Badger Rogue]. As his name suggests, he was notorious for his mischief. In fact, he and his six brothers were so badly behaved that they were all banished from their hometown of Seoul. Though tall and handsome, Osori Jamnom was the worst of the whole bunch; indulging in all sorts of immoral, criminal acts. He travelled and caroused all around the country until all that was left to explore was the Island of Jeju.

He found Jeju much to his liking, and what he liked most was its many women. It wasn't long before a pretty young Haenyeo caught his eye. She was perfect prey for Osori Jamnom for though young, she was already widowed and therefore had no one to protect her from his advances. He followed her home and when night fell, he crept into her bedroom.

오소리 잡놈
The Badger Rogue

The affection of such a creature took a terrible toll on the body of the poor Haenyeo. As each day went by, she grew ever weaker until she was no longer able to go out and catch any seafood. Fortunately, a concerned neighbour alerted the local Shimbang to her sudden illness.

Meanwhile, news of the Osori Jamnom exploits had also reached the ears of his six older brothers. They were all Dokkaebi themselves, also known by the honorific *Yeonggam*/영감 ^{elder} on Jeju, and so they set off to find him in the places where those beings like to dwell. In Jeju this meant:

- ♦ The dense Gotjawal/곶자왈 forests.
- ♦ The rugged Billewat/빌레왓: wild fields strewn with rocks.
- ♦ And the shadows of large boulders (Hanmeodeul/한머들)

But it was among the Oreum/오름^{volcanic hills} that they would find him. As they descended from a particularly high hill, they heard the sounds of Gut/굿^{shamanist ritual}. What really drew their attention was the sound of someone calling their names. The hills echoed with 'Yeonggam, Yeonggam.' This is the first step in the performance of *Yeonggam Noli*/영감 놀이^{elder/Dokkaebi play} performance, Chogamje/초감제: a ritual to summon Yeonggam to the Gutpan/굿판^{place where Gut are conducted}.

Like all of their kind, the six Dokkaebi could not refuse the summons, for they knew what would come next: food and drink. The carousing of the Yeonggam is imitated in the Yeonggam Noli ritual by torch-wielding performers dressed in paper masks, black overcoats and Gat/갓^{wide brimmed hat worn by korean gentlemen}.

The six Yeonggam were not there just to party however. They were also concerned for the young Haenyeo. Seeing how close she was to death, they scolded the Badger Rogue for his reckless behaviour and told him to leave the poor girl at once. This was all it took. He appeared once again in his original form and expressed regret for his possession. The Dokkaebi then told the shaman that if they were treated well, they would actually try and benefit mankind.

At this, the shaman had a feast prepared and so happy were the Dokkaebi that they started to dance. Even the Haenyeo, on the verge of death just a moment before, got up and began dancing with them. Soon the locals all joined in and with the drumming of the junior shamans (Somi/소미) setting a beat, the widow's home was suddenly turned into a merry feasting hall.

Sometime later, the Dokkaebi's attention was drawn elsewhere. Outside they noticed a large straw boat filled with all their favourite food: pork, sorghum rice and sorghum rice cakes. The shaman explained that this was called a Baebangseon/배방선^{a straw boat filled with offerings} and it was prepared specially for them. This is the third step of the ritual, Makpudashi/막푸다시. In this step, the Dokkaebi brothers are encouraged to board a ship along with various other harmful, nameless spirits(Japgwi/잡귀).

Soon, the Dokkaebi were all aboard, and so began the final step of the ritual, Dojin/도진. The Baebangseon, or as it is often called, the '**Ddibae/띠배**^{straw ship}', was cast off and set sail for distant shores. So departed

띠배
Straw Ship

the Dokkaebi and the diseases they brought with them and so began the tradition of the Yeonggam Noli.[120]

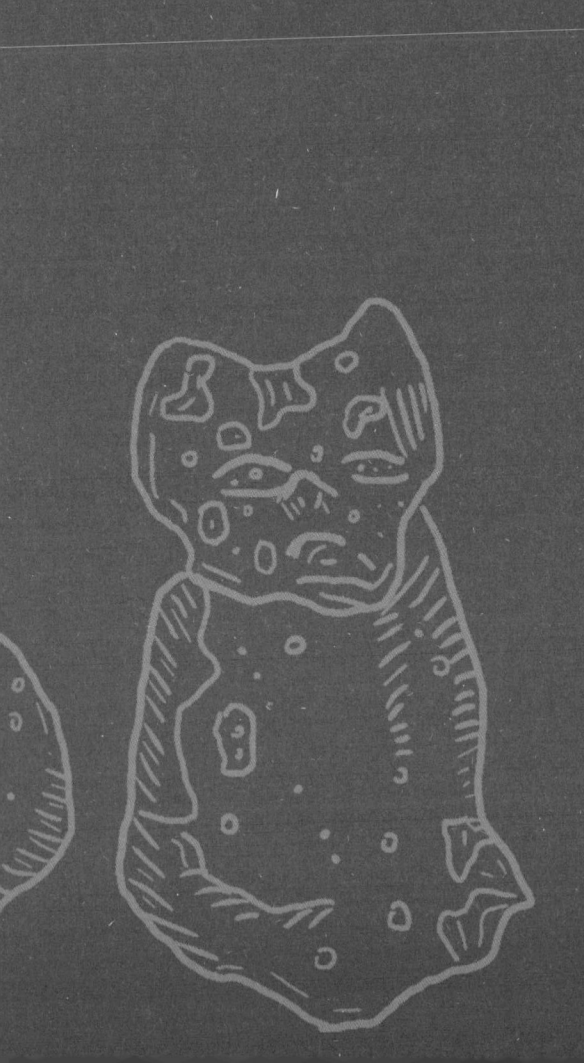

Jeju:

The Island of Coexistence

If even a creature as noxious as the Badger Rogue deserves the right to enjoy a sumptuous feast, then it shows that anyone and anything is welcome in Jeju. Though there are certainly many instances of conflict in the stories we have covered, coexistence is a major theme in Jeju mythology. When the dust has settled, the defeated aggressor is given the chance to go on living and serve a new role, bringing benefit to the world they once terrorised. Gu-Samseung Halmang, who cursed children, now cares for their souls in the Otherworld. Jeongsoonamee, once a danger to his mistress, now serves her as the protector of cows and horses. Even the foreign invader, Kim Tongjeong, was said to have given the islanders something they needed dearly. According to one legend, his final thought just before he fled the island was concern for its inhabitants. To make amends for the trouble he had caused them, he stamped his foot upon a rock on the coast. The rock broke into two and out poured a spring which provides drinking water for the people of Goseong-li/고성리 even to this day.[121]

The greatest testament to the islanders' firm belief in coexistence can be seen in the homes of their gods. If even the two wives of Namseonbi, Yeosan Buin and Noiljedaegwi-il's Daughter, can share a home, then there is surely no rift that cannot be healed.

Yet, it is not merely shamanist gods who can share

the same home. Jeju is a place where even gods from different religions can coexist. Indeed, sometimes all three of the dominant traditional belief systems of the peninsula, that is Shamanism, Buddhism and Confucianism, come together in the worship of a single deity. A prime example of this is the shrine to the five stone Mireuk/미륵 of Hwacheon-dong/화천동 in northern Jeju.

Standing behind the temple of Hwacheonsa/화천사, these five gods appear at first glance to be nothing but rocks. On closer inspection, however, one can make out the features of human faces, simply hewn into natural contours. A pointed head emerges from a rotund mass below, an overhang forms into an aquiline nose. Each statue has an inimitable identity of its own, sculpted as it was by a union between man and nature.

The names of these gods, Mireuk seem to suggest that they are Buddhist in origin. Mireuk after all, as we have seen already, is the Korean name for Maitreya, the Buddha of the future. Moreover, their location behind a Buddhist temple may hint that they are merely an addition to a pre-existing religious complex.

However, these deities actually predate the temple and their names have little to do with the Buddhist understanding of Mireuk. They embody Mireuk as he is seen in Jeju shamanism: a kind of protector Dangshin/ 당신[village god] who also looks after children and aids with their conception and birth. But to complicate matters even further, the ritual held in honour of these Mireuk is neither Buddhist nor shamanist. It takes the form of a Confucian 'Poje/포제 rite'. It is extremely austere, even by Confucian standards, involving none of the fanfare and festivity of shamanist rituals. Only the officiant himself is allowed to participate. Furthermore, during the ritual the statues are adorned with paper hats and clothes to show respect. But in a final twist, though worship of these gods is conducted according to Confucian regulations, the name of their ritual ties them back to Buddhism: the 'Seokbulje/석불제 stone Buddha ritual'.[122]

This single shrine can be seen as a microcosm of both the traditional religious life of Jeju and that of the mainland. Foreign faiths might take root, but the spirit of the Korean people remains. Buddhism adopts native practices willingly and Confucianism, an ideology of the establishment, though resistant to change at first eventually gives way to the will of the people.

As for me, I have fully yielded to the charms of Jeju and Korea. I only hope that their people and gods feel the same way about me. I certainly have no wish to be forced aboard a straw ship any time soon.

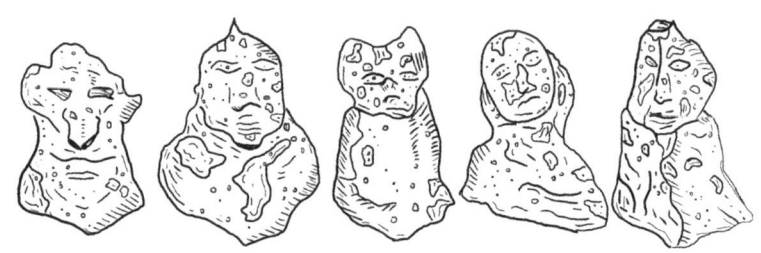

화천사 오신상
The Five Mireuk of Hwacheonsa

Endnotes

1. Kim Hogarth, Hyun-key: 'Gut, the Korean Shamanistic Ritual' (Korean Studies Series No. 43, Jimoondang, 2009), p. 309.
2. 임준성, 「금남최부(錦南崔溥)의 〈탐라시삼십오절(耽羅詩三十五絶)〉 연구」, 한국시가문화연구(구 한국고시가문화연구), 2011, pp. 301-302. Sanbangsan/산방산 is a small mountain in the southwest of Jeju. According to legend, it was once the peak of Hallasan/한라산, the volcano at the centre of Jeju but it was later broken off and thrown to its current location by a god, either the Chinese deity, the Jade Emperor or the island's creator goddess, Seolmundae Halmang/설문대할망. (허남춘,『설문대할망과 제주신화』, 민속원, 2011, p. 35.)
Yuja/유자 and Yugam/유감 are two kinds of citrus fruits native to Jeju.
3. 『고려사』 권 57, 지리지, 전라도 탐라현.
4. 이영권,『제주 역사 기행』, 한겨레신문사, 2004, pp. 59-60.
5. 최열,『옛 그림으로 본 제주』, 혜화 1117, 2021, p. 85.
6. 유홍준,『나의 문화유산답사기-제주편』, 창비, 2012, p. 32.
7. 한진오,『제주 동쪽- 구좌읍, 남원읍, 성산읍, 우도면, 조천읍, 표선면』, 21세기북스, 2021, p. 24.
8. 김유정,『제주 돌담』, 대원사, 2019, pp. 123-124.
9. 김유정, Ibid, p. 125.
10. 송언근,『지리로 가는 제주의 역사, 문화, 생태 탐사』, 교육과학사, 2020, p. 128.
11. 홍죽희, 여연,『제주 당신을 만나다』, 알렙, 2020, p. 15.
12. 송언근,『지리로 가는 제주의 역사, 문화, 생태 탐사』, 교육과학사, 2020 p. 125, 김유정,『제주 돌담』, 대원사, 2019, p. 142.
13. 김유정, Ibid, pp. 144-145.
14. 이윤형, 고광민,『제주의 돌문화』, 제주돌문화공원, 2006, p. 221.
15. Kim, Eugene; Koehler, Robert: 'Joseon's Royal Heritage: 500 Years of Splendor' (Korea Essentials No.7, Seoul Selection, 2011), p. 68.

16 이윤형, 고광민, 『제주의 돌문화』, 제주돌문화공원, 2006, p. 221
17 무라야마 지쥰, 『조선의 귀신』, 문예신서34, 2008, pp. 407-412.
18 김두규, 『우리 풍수 이야기』, 북하우스, 2003, 2012(5쇄), p. 85-89.
19 무라야마 지쥰, 『조선의 귀신』, 문예신서34, 2008, pp. 412-413.
20 강순희, 『제주 신화의 숲』, 한그루, 2022, p. 56.
21 나라키 스에자네, 『조선의 미신과 풍속』, 민속원, 2010, 김희영 옮김, p. 78, p. 97.
22 강순희, 『제주 신화의 숲』, 한그루, 2022, pp. 50-56.
23 최상수, 『세시풍속』, 서문당, 1988, p. 99.
24 정석풍수연구학회, 『풍수 유적 답사기- 감여의 비밀을 찾아서』, 청어람 M&B, 2020, p. 333.
25 Clarissa Wei: 'Where Feeding the Dead is a Fading Tradition' (The New York Times, 2023), https://www.nytimes.com/2023/03/27/dining/tomb-sweeping-day-food.html
26 최상수, 『세시풍속』, 서문당, 1988, pp. 99-101.
27 임승범, 『해원을 위한 저승길 여정』, 민속원, 2021, p. 63.
28 임승범, Ibid, p. 18.
29 진성기, 『제주도 무속논고- 남국의 무속』, 민속원, 2003, p. 45.
30 Also called Songak Gwishin/손각커신 or Cheonyeo Gwishin/처녀귀신.
31 Martin, Diana: 'Chinese Ghost Marriage' (1991, Published in JASO 'Occasional Papers' No. 8), Edited by Hugh D.R. Baker and Stephan Feuchtwang, pp. 25-43, University of Oxford, p. 26.
32 이능화, 『조선무속논고- 역사로 본 한국 무속』, 서영대 옮김, 창비, 2008, 2021(6쇄), p. 329.
33 'Bonpuri' refers to the story of a god's origin in Jeju mythology.
34 lwol/일월 is a special term for 'Ancestor' in Jeju tradition. More specifically, the Hanja character for il/일/日 means 'sun' and the character for wol/월/月 means 'moon.' When used together they convey an idea of eternity, and so serve as a title for an ancestor. The meaning behind this is that like the sun and moon, one's ancestor will exist eternally. From 김순이, 『제주 신화-원형을 살려내고 반듯하게 풀어내다』, 여름 언덕, 2020, p. 377.

35 신예경, 문희숙,『조근조근 제주 신화 2: 자청비부터 도깨비까지, 우리 신화로 배우는 삶과 사랑 이야기』, 지노, 2018, pp. 171-186.
36 현용준,『제주도 신화』, 서문당, 2016(3쇄), pp. 11-21, 여연,『조근조근 제주 신화 1: 천지왕부터 설문대 할망까지, 우리 신화로 배우는 문화 창조 이야기』, 지노, 2018, pp. 20-37, 여름 언덕, 2020, pp. 65-72, 신동흔,『살아있는 우리 신화- 우리 신들의 귀환을 위한 이야기 열두 마당』, 한겨레신문사, 2004, pp. 19-34.
37 Dubois, Thomas A: 'An Introduction to Shamanism' (Cambridge University Press, 2009), p. 83.
38 진성기,『제주도 무속논고- 남국의 무속』, 민속원, 2003, pp. 68-71.
39 여연,『조근조근 제주 신화 1: 천지왕부터 설문대할망까지, 우리 신화로 배우는 문화 창조 이야기』, 지노, 2018, p. 99.
40 진성기, Ibid, p. 70.
41 Chung Myung-sub (Editor): 'Encyclopaedia of Korean Folk Literature Vol III' (The National Folk Museum of Korea, 2014), p. 82.
42 여연,『조근조근 제주 신화 1: 천지왕부터 설문대할망까지, 우리 신화로 배우는 문화 창조 이야기』, 지노, 2018, p. 4.
43 한진오,『모든 것의 처음, 신화』, 한그루, 2019, pp. 33-34.
44 (한국무속학회) 강소전, 심상교, 양종승, 윤동환, 이명숙, 이승범, 최진아, 하효길,『무구의 이해』, 민속원, 2011, pp. 225-226.
45 한진오,『모든 것의 처음, 신화』, 한그루, 2019, p. 37.
46 여연,『조근조근 제주 신화 1: 천지왕부터 설문대할망까지, 우리 신화로 배우는 문화 창조 이야기』, 지노, 2018, p. 105.
47 Yi Yong Bhum: 'Shamanism' in Yi Yong Bhum, Lee Kyung Yup, Choi Jong Seong, Walraven Boudewjin: 'Korean Popular Beliefs' (Jimoondang, 2015), p. 105.
48 Cho, Suk-Joon: 'Korean Administration and Organizational Culture' (Kong and Park USA, 2022), pp. 103-104.
49 Walraven, Boudewijn: 'Popular Religion in a Confucianized Society' in Kim Haboush, Jahyun and Deuchler, Martina: 'Culture and the State in Late Choson Korea' (Harvard University Press, 1999), p. 167.
50 Deuchler, Martina: 'The Confucian Transformation of Korea- A Study

of Society and Ideology' (Harvard University Press, 1992), p. 175.
51 Walraven, Boudewijn: 'Popular Religion in a Confucianized Society' in Kim Haboush, Jahyun and Deuchler, Martina: 'Culture and the State in Late Choson Korea'(Harvard University Press, 1999), pp. 175-177.
52 한승훈,『무당과 유생의 대결』, 도서출판 사우, 2021, p. 8.
53 하순애,『제주도 신당 이야기』, 한그루, 2024(개정판), p. 129.
54 최열,『옛 그림으로 본 제주』, 혜화 1117, 2021, p. 97.
55 최열, Ibid, p. 96.
56 현용준,『제주도 전설』, 서문문고, 1996, 2016(3쇄), pp. 245-246.
57 Tosan is an area on the southeast coast of Jeju.
58 여연,『조근조근 제주 신화 1: 천지왕부터 설문대할망까지, 우리 신화로 배우는 문화 창조 이야기』, 지노, 2018, pp. 223-225, 여연, 문무병,『신화와 함께하는 제주 당올레』, 알렙, 2017, pp. 200-201.
59 진성기,『제주도 무속논고- 남국의 무속』, 민속원, 2002, p. 189.
60 진성기, Ibid, p. 185.
61 여연,『조근조근 제주 신화 3: 가믄장아기부터 강림차사까지, 우리 신화로 배우는 운명과 도전 이야기』, 지노, 2018, pp. 202-204, (한국무속학회) 강소전, 심상교, 양종승, 윤동환, 이명숙, 이승범, 최진아, 하효길『무구의 이해』, 민속원, 2011, p. 208.
62 조성제,『상고사 속의 무속 이야기』, 도서출판 나루터, 2016, pp. 231-233.
63 우종선,『서낭당, 민속예술연구지 제 5 집』, 한국민속극박물관, 2020, p. 51.
64 The gender of the shaman is not mentioned. In many Bonpuri, the gender of characters is not specified. They are merely referred to by their title or profession.
65 The gender of this shaman is also unspecified.
66 여연,『조근조근 제주 신화 1: 천지왕부터 설문대할망까지, 우리 신화로 배우는 문화 창조 이야기』, 지노, 2018, pp. 223-235, 문무병,『신화 함께하는 제주당올레』, 알렙, 2017, pp. 200-207.
67 진성기,『제주도 무속논고- 남국의 무속』, 민속원, 2003, p. 198.

68 현용준,『제주도 신화』, 서문당, 2016(3쇄), pp. 207-209, 진성기, 『제주도 무속논고- 남국의 무속』, 민속원, 2003, pp. 201-202, 허남춘, 『설문대할망과 제주신화』, 민속원, 2011, p. 223, 김순란, 『이토록 신비로운 제주 신화』, 나무늘보, 2017, pp. 163-169.

69 진성기,『1960년대를 중심으로 제주무속학 사진집-1- 복을 비는 사람들』, 도서출판 디딤돌, 2008, pp. 67-68.

70 진성기, Ibid, pp. 67-68.

71 한진오,『모든 것의 처음, 신화』, 한그루, 2019, p. 293.

72 허남춘,『설문대할망과 제주신화』, 민속원, 2017, p. 150.

73 신예경, 문희숙,『조근조근 제주 신화 2: 자청비부터 도깨비까지, 우리 신화로 배우는 삶과 사랑 이야기』, 지노, 2018, pp. 228-229.

74 신예경, 문희숙, Ibid, p. 191-213, 김수란,『이토록 신비로운 제주신화』, 나무늘보. 2017, pp. 151-160, 한진오,『모든 것의 처음, 신화』, 한그루, 2019, p. 292, 현용준,『제주도 신화』, 서문당, 2016(3쇄), pp. 182-198.

75 나라키 스에자네,『조선의 미신과 풍속』, 민속원, 2010, 김희영 옮김, p. 59.

76 고제희,『대한민국 1% 부자의 길로 가는 시크릿 풍수』, 북이십일, 2020, p. 193.

77 Or is he still alive now?

78 김수란,『이토록 신비로운 제주 신화』, 나무늘보, 2017, pp. 117-121, 현용준,『제주도 신화』, 서문당, 2016 (3쇄), pp. 133-141, 문희숙, 신예경,『조근조근 제주 신화 2: 자청비부터 도깨비까지, 우리 신화로 배우는 삶과 사랑 이야기』, 지노, 2018, pp. 153-165.

79 현용준, Ibid, pp. 87-133, 여연,『조근조근 신화 3: 가믄장아기부터 강림차사까지, 우리 신화로 배우는 운명과 도전 이야기』, 지노, 2018, pp. 57-134, 신동흔,『살아있는 우리 신화- 우리 신들의 귀환을 위한 이야기 열두 마당』, 한겨레신문사, 2004, 한겨레신문사, pp. 140-161.

80 Kim Seong-Nae: 'Shamanic Epics and Narrative Construction of Identity on Cheju Island' (Asian Folklore Studies, Vol. 63, No. 1 (2004), p. 60.

81 유홍준, 『나의 문화유산답사기- 제주편』, 2012, 창비, p. 37.
82 여연, 문무병, 『신화와 함께하는 제주 당올레』, 알렙, 2017, pp. 17-27. 홍죽희, 여연, 『제주 당신을 만나다』, 알렙, 2020, pp. 166-169. 여연, 『조근조근 제주 신화 1: 천지왕부터 설문대할망까지, 우리 신화로 배우는 문화 창조 이야기』, 지노, 2018, pp. 187-206. 현용준, 『제주도 전설』, 서문문고, 1996, 2016(3쇄), pp. 246-248. 김순이, 『제주 신화- 원형을 살려내고 반듯하게 풀어내다』, 여름 언덕, 2020, pp. 327-338.
83 David J. Nemeth (권상철 옮김): 'Rediscovering Hallasan- Jeju Island's Traditional Landscape of Sincerity, Mysticism and Adventure(신비, 성실, 모험의 제주 전통 경관)' (purungil/푸른길, 2019), p. 52.
84 Sanshin Baekgwan is not the name of a single god. There are many Sanshin Baekgwan/산신백관 enshrined all over the island.
85 문무병, 『제주의 성숲 당올레 111』, 황금알, 2020, p. 188.
86 홍죽희, 여연, 『제주 당신을 만나다』, 알렙, 2020, pp. 137-140.
87 인성리 방사탑 2호/ Inseong-ri Bangsatab No, 2 (Jeju Special Self-Governing Province Folk Cultural Heitage No. B-17)
88 용수마을 방사탑 2호 / Yongsu Maeul Bangsatap No. 2 (Jeju Special Self-Governing Province Folk Cultural Heitage No. 8-9)
89 고제희, 『대한민국 1% 부자의 길로 가는 시크릿 풍수』, 북이십일, 2020, p. 127.
90 Rhie, Jong-Chul et al: 'Changsung' (Youlhwadang, 3rd printing, 2005), p. 131.
91 김영돈, 『제주 성읍 마을』, 대원사, 2012, p. 78.
92 김영돈, Ibid, p. 78.
93 김영돈, Ibid, p. 75.
94 이종철, 『한국 민속신앙의 탐구』, 민속원, 2009, pp. 173-178.
95 Lee, Peter, Ch'oe, Yeongcho and De Bary, Theodore (Editors): 'Sources of Korean Tradition, Volume 1: From Early Times through the Sixteenth Century' (Columbia University Press, 1997), p. 203.
96 Story collected from 애월면 광령리 고인훈씨 분친, 현용준, 『제주도 전설』, 서문문고, 1996, 2016(3쇄), p. 101.

97　홍죽희, 여연,『제주 당신을 만나다』, 알렙, 2020, pp. 185-189.
98　홍죽희, 여연, Ibid, pp. 186-187.
99　우종선,『서낭당, 민속예술연구지 제 5 집』, 한국민속극박물관, 2020, p. 81.
100　한진오,『제주 동쪽- 구좌읍, 남원읍, 성산읍, 우도면, 조천읍, 표선면』, 21세기북스, 2021, p. 70.
101　한진오,『모든 것의 처음, 신화』, 한그루, 2019, p. 154.
102　한진오, Ibid, p. 98. Chung Myung-sub (Editor): 'Encyclopaedia of Korean Folk Literature Vol III' (The National Folk Museum of Korea, 2014), p. 309.
103　김순이,『제주 신화- 원형을 살려내고 반듯하게 풀어내다』, 여름언덕, 2020, pp. 299-315.
104　허남춘,『설문대할망과 제주신화』, 민속원, 2017, p. 234.
105　김수란,『이토록 신비로운 제주 신화』, 나무늘보, 2017, pp. 39-47. 김순이,『제주 신화- 원형을 살려내고 반듯하게 풀어내다』, 여름언덕, 2020, pp. 73-86. 현용준,『제주도 신화』, 서문당, 2016(3쇄), pp. 32-35. 조현설,『우리 신화의 수수께끼』, 한겨레 출판, 2005, pp. 62-66. 신동흔,『살아있는 우리 신화- 우리 신들의 귀환을 위한 이야기 열두 마당』, 한겨레신문사, 2004, pp. 66-79.
106　문희숙, 신예경,『조근조근 제주 신화 2: 자청비부터 도깨비까지, 우리 신화로 배우는 삶과 사랑 이야기』, 지노, 2018, pp. 38-39, p. 47.
107　허남춘,『설문대할망과 제주신화』, 민속원, 2011, p. 193.
108　What these five grains actually are varies considerably. The most common conception of the 'Five Grains' are however: rice/쌀, (soy) beans/콩, fox tail millet/조, common millet/기장 and barley/보리. From 김호숙, 마석한,『고조선과 동이- 사기, 한서, 삼국지, 후한서로 읽어 보는』, 한국학술정보, 2022, p. 35. More generally though the term 'Five Grains' can also refer to all grains or staple crops.
109　신예경, 문희숙,『조근조근 제주 신화 2: 자청비부터 도깨비까지, 우리 신화로 배우는 삶과 사랑 이야기』, 지노, 2018, pp. 51-135. 신동흔,『살아있는 우리 신화- 우리 신들의 귀환을 위한 이야기

열두 마당』, 한겨레 신문사, 2004, pp. 222-250. 김순이,『제주 신화- 원형을 살려내고 반듯하게 풀어내다』, 여름 언덕, 2020, pp. 201-244. 김익두,『한국신화를 찾아 떠나는 여행- 우리 문화의 근원, 그 오래된 미래의 탐구』, 지식산업사, 2021, pp. 282-304.

110 여연,『조근조근 신화 3: 가믄장아기부터 강림차사까지, 우리 신화로 배우는 운명과 도전 이야기』, 지노, 2018, pp. 162-163.

111 김순이,『제주 신화- 원형을 살려내고 반듯하게 풀어내다』, 여름언덕, 2020, pp. 317-325. 한진오,『모든 것의 처음, 신화』, 한그루, 2019, p. 185. 국립제주박물관,『태풍 고백- 하나의 눈동자를 가진 외눈박이 바람의 고백』, 국립제주박물관, 2020, p. 110.

112 한진오, Ibid, pp. 117-119.

113 김유정,『제주 돌담』, 대원사, 2019, p. 86.

114 여연,『조근조근 신화 3: 가믄장아기부터 강림차사까지, 우리 신화로 배우는 운명과 도전 이야기』, 지노, 2018, p. 172. 고광민,『마라도의 역사와 민속』, 한그루, 2007, p.165.

115 홍죽희, 여연,『제주 당신을 만나다』, 알렙, 2020, pp. 29-32 and a piece of paper recording the Bonpuri which was left in a jar at the shrine, entitled: 김녕 서문하르방당 본풀이 provided by 파평윤씨 제주도문중 회장 교육학박사 윤두호

116 김삼룡,『미륵불』, 대원사, 2011, pp. 13-15.

117 김광언,『풍수지리(집과마을)』, 대원사, 1993, p. 43.

118 김선현,『컬러가 내 몸을 바꾼다』, 넥서스 Books, 2009, pp. 67-68.

119 신예경, 문희숙,『조근조근 제주 신화 2: 자청비부터 도깨비까지, 우리 신화로 배우는 삶과 사랑 이야기』, 지노, 2018, pp. 233-236. 여연, 문무병,『신화 함께하는 제주 당올레』, 알렙, 2017, pp. 174-176.

120 김종대,『한국 민간신앙의 전승과 그 의미』, 민속원, 2021, pp. 229-233. 신예경, 문희숙,『조근조근 제주 신화 2: 자청비부터 도깨비까지, 우리 신화로 배우는 삶과 사랑 이야기』, 지노, 2018, pp. 237-245.

121 현용준,『제주도 전설』, 서문문고, 1996, 2016(3쇄), pp. 95-99.

122 이영권,『제주 역사 기행』, 한겨레신문사, 2004, pp. 186-187.

Index

This book is based on the card game of the same name created by author Tom Borelli. Let's enjoy together with the 52 Jeju myth cards that appear in the game.

Green Household Card
Sandam
산담 32-35
Gopang
고팡 73-75, 88
Jeongjumok and Jeongnang
정주목과 정낭 81-83
Jeongji
정지 85-86
Sangbang
상방 87
Haunted House
흉가 88-89

Yellow Household God Card
Anchilseong
안칠성 72-75
Jumokjishin
주목지신 78-81
Jowang Halmang
조왕할망 85-86, 98
Munjeonshin
문전신 87-88, 98

Red Guardian Spirit Cards
Bangool Poom
방울품 69-71
Chilseong-shinsang and Heomeng-ee doll
칠성신상과 허멩이 인형 66-69
Yeongjip
영집 51-54
Shinsomi
신소미 135-136
Skull of Samanee's Ancestor
사만이 조상의 해골 94-97
Ganglim
강림 97-101
Yeongdeung Halmang
영등할망 28, 150-154
Straw ship
띠배 171-172, 178
Bangsatap
방사탑 108-111
Dolhareubang
돌하르방 110-113, 116
Coral Haenyeo
산호 해녀 122

Samseung Halmang
삼승할망 130-135
Gwangyangdangshin
광양당신 118-121
Jacheongbi
자청비 140-144, 150
Mireukdol
미륵돌 158-161, 164
Blood of a White Horse and
Sorghum Rice
백마 피와 수수밥 164-168

Black Harmful Spirit Card
Resentful Ancestor Spirit
조상원귀 39-40
Hanyangilwol
한양일월 41-43
Sumyeongjangja's Household
수명장자의 집 44-47
King Seosoo's Daughter
서수왕 따님아기 144-147
Aegi-oepgae
애기업개 156-158
Cheongu-agoo-daemeng-ee
천구아구대멩이 62-63, 153
Gwayangsaengee Couple
과양생이 부부 98-100
Waenoonbegi
외눈배기 151-153
Hol-eomongdol
홀어멍돌 154-155
Noiljedaegwi-il's Daughter
노일제대귀일의 딸 78-86, 145
Sanshin Baekgwan of Gonaebong
고내봉의 산신백관 107-108

Gu-Samseung Halmang
구삼승할망 132-134, 176
The Badger Rogue
오소리 잡놈 169-170, 176
Jeongsoonamee Owl
정수남이 부엉이 141-146, 176
Socheonguk
소천국 104-106, 118
Kim Tongjeong
김통정 116-118, 176
Jang Gilson
장길손 124-126, 130

Blue Special Ability Card
Encroaching Roots
침입하는 뿌리 34
Bone Infesting Insects
뼈에 들끓는 벌레 37
Moving the Grave
이장 36
Weeding the Grave
벌초 38-39
Shimbang
심방 50-54, 60, 71, 169
Sam-mengdoo
삼멩두 53-54
Magistrate Lee Hyeongsang
이형상 목사 58-60
Magistrate Yang
양씨 목사 60-63

Written and Illustrated by Tom Borrelli

After studying history at Kings College London, Tom Borrelli came to Korea where he has lived for more than eight years. Teaching English and History for seven of those years, and studying Korean at Seoul National University for the other, he has fallen in love with Korea's history and traditions. For the past four years, he has been living on Jeju Island, where he has made it his mission to find and catalogue all of the island's shrines and their gods. As of now, the number of shrines he has visited stands at just over 150.

Mail. tombowewe@live.co.uk

Reviewed by Cho Kyungcheol

Historian. He has been teaching Korean history at Yonsei University since 2003 and directs The institute for the historical Appeliation of Kingdoms[Nations]. He is the author of titles such as '*My Own Korean History*,' '*Research on the History of Buddhism in Baekje*,' and '*Gaze of Artefacts - Stone*,' and has published over 50 research papers. He continuously seeks new historical perspectives.

Mail. 12061289yu@gmail.com

Translation Proofread by Hwang Jaun

Ewha Graduate School of Translation and Interpretation, MA. Primarily focusing on art and media translation, with the hope that meaningful artworks spread their wings and connect with a wider world through translation.

Mail. fromjaun@gmail.com

Supervised and Summarised in Korean by Cho Buyong

She worked as a film journalist for four years and is currently exploring Korean artefacts to develop content, which she introduces through publications and on the web. She has published 'The Animal Encyclopedia of the Baekje Gilt-Bronze Incense Burner' and 'Gaze of Artefacts - Stone,' and runs the Korean history newsletter 'My Own Korean History Letters.'

Ghosts and Gods of Tamna : The Eternal Guardians of Jeju
탐라의 귀신: 제주의 영원한 수호자들

Copyright © 2024 by Tom Borrelli
All rights reserved. No part of this book may be reproduced or used in any manner without the written permission of both the copyright owner and the publisher, except for the use of quotations in a book review.

Published by Yumool-siseon, Gyeonggi-do

First Edition

Email. yumooleyes@gmail.com
Instagram. @yumool_eyes
X. @my_k_history

Written by Tom Borrelli
Illustrated by Tom Borrelli
Supervised and Summarised in Korean by Cho Buyong
Translation Proofread by Hwang Jaun
Reviewed by Cho Kyungcheol
Edited by Cho Buyong and Cho Buna
Designed by Nam Seonmi and Nam Yeonju

ISBN 979-11-980204-2-0 (03910)
Printed in the Republic of Korea